ESSENTIALS
LEARN TO PLAY
GUITAR

E S S E N T I A L S

LEARN TO PLAY
GUITAR

igloo

Published by Igloo Books Limited
Garrard Way, Kettering
Northants, NN16 8PX
www.igloo-books.com

This edition published 2006

ISBN 1-84561-154-3

Project management: Kandour Ltd

Editorial and design management: Emma Hayley and Jenny Ross
Author: Jeff Ellis
Text design and layout: Chris Readlamb
Cover design: Chris Readlamb
Cover image: David Wright
Illustrations: Jeff Ellis, Chris Readlamb
Photography: David Wright
With thanks to: Steve Jolly & staff, Holiday Music Ltd,
396-398 High Road, Leytonstone, London E11, UK
Also thanks to: Matthew Cang, Andy Sleigh, Celestine Laporte,
Jane Laporte and Josephine Bacon

Contents

Introduction

Whether you want to learn a few simple guitar chords to play at home or you dream of becoming a lead guitarist, this step-by-step guide will set you confidently on the road to achieving your goal. We'll guide you through basic chords and fingering techniques, cover music theory, and advise you about buying equipment.

But before we look at how to play the guitar we need to spend some time looking at the instrument itself.

You'll need to be able to recognize and name the different parts of the guitar in order to follow this book, so first let's take a look at each element of the instrument, including types and weights of strings.

We'll learn the names of the strings, along with some of the notes on the neck of the guitar, which will make the final step of tuning the guitar easier. Once this is achieved you will be ready to begin playing.

Guitar

In this book we'll be concentrating on steel strung guitars, from electric to acoustic and those somewhere in-between.

We'll begin by looking at some of the types of guitar available. More information can be found in Chapter Seven, which covers buying guitars.

Guitars fall into two broad categories, acoustic and electric. Acoustic guitars produce the sound themselves, whereas electric guitars require some form of amplification for the sound to be heard.

Within these two categories there are many different types and styles of guitar.

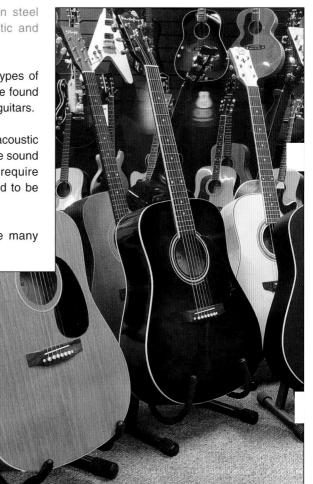

Right: A variety of guitars on display

Acoustic guitars

These guitars are based on the original type that evolved from smaller instruments like the lute.

The acoustic guitar has a hollow box for a body with a hole under the strings. This allows the sound from the resonating strings to bounce around inside the guitar body and be amplified.

The nylon strings and slightly smaller body shape define classical-style acoustic guitars. This gives the sound they produce a quieter and softer tone. The necks of these guitars are slightly wider and shorter than other acoustic types and the front of the neck where the fingers are placed is flatter than in other guitars. This favors a style of playing where picking at individual notes is the priority rather than strumming chords.

*The word **guitarra** can be traced back to 13th century Spain and is thought to have come from the Arabic word* qitara, *meaning "stringed instrument." Images of people playing guitar-like instruments have been found that date back thousands of years to ancient Egypt.*

Far Left: Acoustic guitars
Left: The sound hole of an acoustic guitar

There are also arch-top guitars that have curved tops similar in design to violins or cellos. This type of guitar is not very common and is usually more expensive than other types.

Spanish guitars are very similar to classical guitars but tend to have a sharper and brighter sound to them.

This does not mean that classical or Spanish guitars cannot be used to learn on but you may have to work harder to form chords and your finger technique will feel slightly different when you try other types of guitars.

Flat-top acoustic guitars are the most common type of acoustic found and are so-called because of the flatness of the wood that forms the top part of the body, the front of the guitar, where the hole is.

Right: A classical guitar
Far Right: A flat-top acoustic

Flat tops come in many different sizes. The size and depth of the body has an effect on the sound produced by the guitar. Larger bodies generally produce deeper tones but the type of wood and construction methods used will also affect this.

The largest flat-top guitars are referred to as Dreadnoughts.

Flat-top guitars usually have steel strings, which produce a brighter, louder tone. The neck of the guitar is narrower than that of classical and Spanish guitars and has a rod running inside the length of the neck to give it the extra strength needed for the tension of steel strings.

Resonator guitars are similar to flat-tops but have a metal resonator plate attached to the body rather than a sound hole. The purpose of this is to create a louder sound than is possible with a normal acoustic guitar. This was important to guitarists before the electric guitar was invented, as it was often hard for the guitar to be heard above other instruments in a band. These guitars are still occasionally used in blues or country bands.

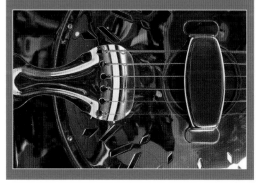

Twelve-string guitars are similar to their six-string relatives but have a wider neck to accommodate the extra strings. They are played in a similar way to six-string guitars as the strings are set in pairs and usually tuned so that each pair is the same note but an octave apart, giving one a higher sound—except for the top two, which are the same (see Chapter Six for further explanation of musical notes). The second string in each pair is also thinner than the first.

Above Left: A resonator plate

Electric guitars

Electric guitars usually have solid wooden bodies and produce very little sound unless connected to an amplifier and speakers. Instead of using a sound box to amplify the sound, magnetic pickups detect the vibration of the strings and convert them into electrical signals.

By far the most common electric guitar shapes available are the classic ones that have survived since the Fifties and Sixties and have been proven to be both comfortable and effective to play.

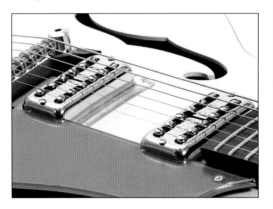

These signals travel along a cable connected to an amplifier that can modify the signal to drive speakers and it is the rapid movement of the speaker cones moving backward and forward that produces the sound.

Electric guitars come in many shapes and sizes because the shape of the body has little effect on the sound, although it is important that the body has the strength to handle the tension of the strings. It is possible to have a guitar made to almost any shape you wish.

Right: The magnetic pickups of an electric guitar
Far Right: Electric guitars come in many shapes

Some of the most famous designs have particular features and qualities to them that help to endear them to different musicians. For example, guitar-maker Fender has two main guitar designs—the *Telecaster* and *Stratocaster* —that have remained largely the same for decades.

The *Telecaster*, or *Tele* for short, has two pickups along the body to detect the sound and is suited to rhythm guitarists, while the *Stratocaster* or *Strat* has three pickups allowing for more tonal variety. The Strat also has a cutaway design along the bottom half of the body that allows players to reach higher notes along the neck. It also has an arm that allows the player to stretch the strings and alter the notes. These features make the Strat a favorite among lead guitarists.

The other major player in guitar manufacturing, Gibson, also has two main designs that feature similar qualities to attract different types of players. The *Gibson SG* has a classic devil's horns shape to the body and has two pickups. Gibson's pickups are larger than Fender's as each one is actually a double pickup. Rhythm players tend to favor the *SG* over Gibson's other designs.

Gibson entices lead guitarists with its *Les Paul*

Left: A Fender *Telecaster* and Gibson *Les Paul*

guitar. It has a distinctive body shape with an extreme cutaway shape that allows easy access to the highest of possible notes. The body has a gentle curve to its surface unlike the flat designs of most bodies.

There are distinct tonal qualities to Gibson and Fender guitars because of the placement and type of pickups used on them, though the look of the guitar will have an impact on why a person buys a particular brand.

Between the acoustic and electric guitars come the hybrids: the electro-acoustic guitars and semi-acoustic guitars.

Semi-acoustic guitars

A semi-acoustic guitar is basically an electric guitar with a hollow body—this gives the instrument some acoustic ability. Although this means that they can be played without electric amplification, the sound they produce without it is still not very loud. The purpose of the hollow body is to give the guitar a warmer sound and to affect what the pickups send to the amp. Semi-acoustics usually have larger bodies; the Gretsch guitar is a famous example of this design.

Right: A Gretsch semi-acoustic guitar

Electro-acoustic guitars

Electro-acoustic guitars are acoustic guitars that have some way of amplifying their sound. This is done either by having a pickup, microphone, or both fitted to the guitar along with volume and tone controls.

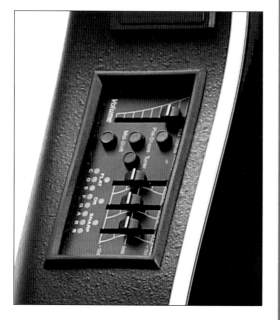

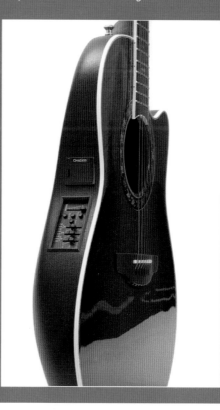

Note that electro-acoustic guitars are usually designed to sound best when amplified and may not have the same quality of tone as a normal flat-top guitar when played acoustically, but they certainly sound better unplugged than semi-acoustics.

Far Left: The volume and tone controls on an electro-acoustic guitar
Left: An Ovation guitar

Guitar parts

Let's now look at the main parts of the guitar and their functions.

The body

The body is the largest single part of the guitar and the look of it is often what first attracts a potential buyer. Be it the shape, the color, the type of material it is made from, or a combination of these, it is the body that defines the character of the guitar.

For acoustic guitars, it is the body that produces the sound, so the type of wood and the way it is constructed are more important than for electric guitars.

Acoustic guitars are often made from woods such as spruce, cedar, or mahogany, although many more are made of layers of different woods called laminates.

It is most important that the top of the body is made from good-quality material as the majority of the sound is produced by this part as it transfers the vibrations of the strings to the rest of the body. The top piece of the body is called the soundboard.

Right: Semi-acoustic guitar bodies
Far Right: The internal struts of an acoustic add strength to the body

The body is held together internally by bracing struts. These produce the strength the body needs to stand up to the immense stress caused by highly tensioned strings. The size and placement of these struts has some effect on the overall tone of the guitar.

The body of an electric guitar is usually made of solid wood and so the type of wood used has less effect on the tone of the guitar than in acoustic guitars. The solid body is rarely cut from a single piece of wood, as joining various hardwoods together usually produces a much stronger instrument. Many electric guitars are made of inexpensive wood such as ash and then topped with a thin layer of more attractive or better quality wood.

The body has the neck and bridge of the guitar fitted to it. Electric guitar bodies also have channels and slots carved into them to take the wiring, switches, and knobs that are essential for controlling the sound.

The scratch-plate

The scratch-plate is attached to the top face of the body and is usually made of laminated plastic. On electric guitars, pickups or controls may also be mounted on it.

Its purpose is to protect the wood and lacquered finish of the body from damage caused by strumming.

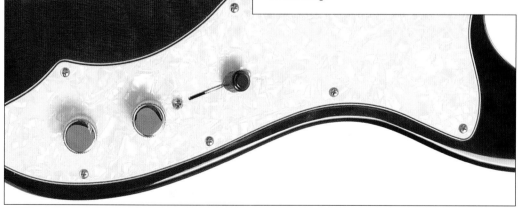

Left: A scratch-plate protects the wood of the guitar body

The bridge

At its most basic, the bridge is what holds one end of the string to the body. The strings are usually threaded through the back of the bridge and held in place by the ring attached to the end of the string, catching against holes at the back.

A lot of electric guitars thread their strings through the back of the body and into the rear of the bridge. The bridge on an electric guitar is usually height-adjustable. This changes the height of the strings—a process called raising or lowering the action. Some bridges also have adjustments that allow for fine-tuning of the strings. Other bridges are spring-loaded at the back to allow for the use of tremolo arms or whammy bars. These bars allow for notes to be bent or detuned by stretching the strings.

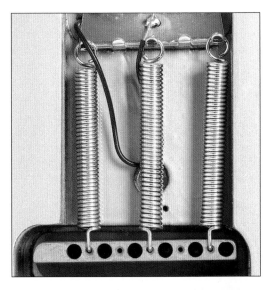

Top: The tension springs of a Fender *Stratocaster*
Bottom: The bridge of an acoustic

The pickups

Pickups are fitted to all electric and semi-acoustic guitars and most electro-acoustics as well. However, some electro-acoustics have small condenser microphones or a combination of both pickups and microphones.

Pickups are made of magnets (usually one per string) and coils of wire. Vibrations in the string are detected by the magnets and translated into electric current by the wire coils; the signal is then sent to the amplifier via the guitar lead.

Most electric guitars have at least two pickups. The pickups are positioned on the body so that they pick out different tones from each other. Pickups positioned toward the rear of the guitar give a treble-rich tone while those positioned toward the neck give warmer bass tones.

Switches and knobs

If you have pickups on a guitar then you will at least have a volume control and a tone control that allows for bass and treble settings. If you have more than one pickup you will also have a switch that lets you choose which pickup is activated or allows you to use all of them.

You may also have space for a battery and a power switch. This is to power a pre-amplifier that enables the guitar to produce greater volume. There is sometimes a small LED-type light to show if it is switched on. Don't forget to change the battery regularly and carry a spare.

Tonal position

Changing the tone of the guitar between bass and treble sounds using pickups is not the only way of achieving tonal effects. You can also adjust the position of the hand you use to play the strings. Moving the position of this hand toward the rear of the body will create a thinner sound with more treble in it and moving the hand toward the neck creates a chunkier sound with more bass tones.

Far Left: A pickup is a series of magnets
Left: The volume and tone controls of an electric guitar

The neck

The neck is attached to the body of the guitar with strong glue, bolts, or both and a lot of pressure is placed upon this join by the tension of the strings.

The neck must be made from sturdy wood, as the pressure on it is likely to twist and bend it; this is something to look out for when buying a guitar, old or new.

Changes in humidity and temperature can also affect the straightness of the neck.

The truss rod

Right: The neck of an acoustic guitar
Far Right: The truss rod allows for small adjustments to the neck

Inside the neck of steel-strung guitars lies a metal truss rod that helps keep the neck in shape. The rod runs from top to bottom and usually has a bolt at one end to allow for minor corrections to straighten the neck. You should be very careful if you attempt to do this yourself. It is best performed by a skilled craftsman.

The fretboard

The flat face of the neck has another piece of wood attached to it where the guitarist's fingers run up and down. This is called the fretboard and can be made from a different type of wood from the rest of the neck. It's usually made of rosewood, maple, or ebony.

needed to hold the string down and changes to finger positions can be quicker. Care must be taken when adjusting the action or the strings may buzz against the frets.

The frets

The fretboard has metal strips called frets that are embedded and slightly raised above the fretboard. The strings are pressed against these to sound the different notes.

The height of the string above the fret is called "the action" and, the smaller this distance, the easier it is to play because less pressure is

Frets are usually made from nickel alloy and often wear out with heavy use—fortunately they are quite easy to replace.

The spacing between frets is crucial to the tuning of the guitar—the frets gradually get closer together the further you move up the neck toward the body. The 12th fret is exactly halfway along the length of the string and is the one with double dots on it. The significance of the 12th fret will be addressed later in the book.

Left: Nickel alloy frets are embedded in the fretboard

The inlays

The headstock

Inlaid along the fretboard at specific points are dots to help the player work out the position of various notes. These dots may be in the shape of diamonds, squares, numbers, or other symbols. They can also be made of various materials such as wood, plastic, or mother-of-pearl. Inexpensive guitars sometimes just use paint but almost any material can be used.

The inlays are always on the 3rd, 5th, 7th, 9th, 12th, 15th, 17th, 19th, and 21st frets. As mentioned previously, the 12th fret has a double inlay. If the neck reaches the 24th fret, there will be a double inlay there as well.

The headstock is positioned at the end of the neck. It is also referred to as the head and can be shaped in various ways to facilitate tuning. Some modern guitars do not have a head, to help reduce the weight of the guitar. The strings are then tuned at the back of the bridge instead.

Right: An ornate inlay in the fretboard
Far Right: The headstock of a Fender *Telecaster*

The nut

The machine heads

The machine heads are the tuners of the guitar. By turning them, you adjust the tension of the string and raise or lower the pitch of each string.

Some machine heads are completely sealed, while others are either open at the back or covered with a cap. All of them usually allow some access for lubrication and most have some way of tightening and loosening the stiffness of the twisting action.

Just before the start of the head, there is a strip of grooved plastic, bone, graphite, or other hard material that marks the zero position of the strings. The other end of the string is at the bridge, with the halfway point being the 12th fret.

Far Left: The nut is often made of hard plastic
Left: An ornate machine head on an acoustic guitar

The capstan

The capstan is the part of the machine head that protrudes through the front of the headstock. A capstan has either a hole or a slot cut into it for threading the string.

Capstans are slightly concave in shape to help the strings curl neatly around them. Neat winding of the strings helps to keep tuning accurate as overlapping winds of the string can slip and ruin the tuning of the instrument.

Right: The concave shape of a capstan
Far Right: Varieties of strings
Facing Page: Each string on a guitar is of a different thickness

The strings

Nylon strings are mainly used on classical or Spanish-style guitars. These types of guitars used to use strings made of catgut, a material made from the intestines of sheep or horses—not cats!

Steel strings are the main focus of this book and they are usually coated in nickel. Steel strings for acoustic guitars are sometimes coated in bronze to give a warmer, richer sound.

Most strings are of a standard length but you can also get shorter strings for short-neck or junior guitars.

Strings come in sets of six and each is of a different thickness. The thinner the string, the higher the note it is used for. The thicker strings have tight windings of steel around them with either a round or flat finish to them.

The ends of the strings are usually twisted around rings called barrels that stop the string pulling through the holes in the bridge. Some strings end in a nipple of metal and are referred to as bullet strings. These strings are meant for guitars that have whammy bars or tremolo arms and help to keep them in tune under the extra stress.

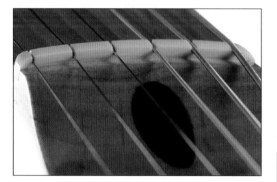

The sets of strings themselves come in different thicknesses called gauges with sizes measured in thousandths of an inch. Sets of strings are sold by gauge and come in heavy, medium, light, and ultra-light gauge.

Lighter gauge strings require slightly less effort to play and bend but are easier to snap. Heavier strings require more tension to tune and sound louder. Light-gauge strings are regarded as standard and come fitted on most guitars.

Even within the different gauges there is some variety of weight or thickness. This is usually referred to by the diameter of the thinnest string within the gauge, called the first string. On light strings, this can be between .009 and .011 of an inch. Ultra-light strings can go down to around .007.

It might be worth trying out medium strings if you want to achieve a louder, heavier sound from your guitar.

Changing the strings

Guitar strings should be replaced regularly. They are one of the least expensive components of the guitar but have a major effect on the overall quality of the sound. The lifetimes of strings vary, depending on a number of factors, including how old they are, how often the guitar is played, how

Plectrums

Although not technically part of the guitar, plectrums or picks, as they are sometimes called, have to be considered in order to protect your nails while strumming the guitar.

Plectrums come in a wide variety of shapes and sizes and are usually made from nylon. They are pointed at the end that strikes the strings.

Plectrums also come in different thicknesses and are measured in hundredths of a millimeter. Thinner ones are more flexible and heavier ones tend to be used with heavier gauge strings that require more force to play them. Which you use is largely a matter of choice and can depend on such factors as how big your fingers are and how much force you use to play. The easiest way to find your favorite is to buy a selection and try them out.

heavily the strings have been played and the conditions to which they have been exposed, such as dampness or dust.

Strings should be replaced if you can see changes in color along the string or if you can see damage to the tight coils of the thicker strings.

Ideally, strings should be changed one at a time so that the neck remains under constant tension. There will be times, though, when you will want to remove all the strings at once to clean the fretboard, as this area can become very soiled.

Don't leave a guitar without strings for any length of time as the neck will resettle and change its shape and the action may never be the same. Take care when changing strings for the first few times as it is fairly easy to hurt yourself with the end of a string.

Remove the old strings by unwinding them rather than cutting them off with wire cutters. Once they are unwound from the machine heads, you can then cut the curled ends off to make unthreading the bridge easier. It is usual to replace the thicker strings first and work toward the thinnest one.

New strings come coiled in individual envelopes. It is best to lay them out in order first. There is usually a guide on the package to help you identify the strings. Carefully uncoil the new string, avoiding putting any bends or kinks in it.

Thread it through the bridge and pull it up the length of the neck to the machine head, where you thread it through the capstan. You will need to leave some slack on the string so you can coil it enough times around the capstan to stop the string slipping when you play it.

Right: Thread the string through the capstan
Far Right: Some electric guitars thread strings through the back of the body

The thicker strings need fewer coils to maintain pressure than thinner ones, three or four times around the capstan should do it. If you leave around 4inches (10cm) at the bottom of each string, this should give you enough length for winding.

Stringing guitars can be quite tricky at first, as the strings tend to slip from the capstan when you are winding them. After a little practice, you should find a technique for doing it successfully.

It will be easier if you put a sharp bend in the thicker strings at the capstan before winding starts. Then use your thumb or finger to press the string down on the headstock to maintain tension while winding the machine head. Try to keep the coils tidy, as this will help prevent string slippage later.

When the string is fully wound, give it a few gentle pushes between the nut and the capstan to settle the string and its coils.

The thinner strings are more difficult to keep in place and have a greater tendency to slip while being wound. Some people create a simple knot around the capstan to help, though this makes removing the string slightly harder. It can be a useful trick, however, when you first start out but will make changing a string during a performance more time-consuming.

Top: Give the string a sharp bend around the capstan
Middle: Acoustic guitars have pegs that hold the strings in place
Bottom: Use your finger to maintain the tension of the string

Tuning the guitar

Once the strings are threaded and settled, you can tidy the ends of the strings by clipping them back to the capstan. This will help you avoid the inevitable scratches you might otherwise get from them. Cable-cutters and side-cutters are good tools for this but old nail-clippers will do.

Right: Clip the strings back to the capstan
Far Right: A digital tuner

Now that you have restrung the guitar, it is time to tune it.

It is important to get the tuning of your guitar right as it will help you with your learning if you can get used to hearing sounds the way they are meant to be. It is even more important if you are going to play along with other musicians. Tuning is normally performed on open strings, which means that the full length of the string is allowed to resonate without any fingers on the frets.

Types of tuners

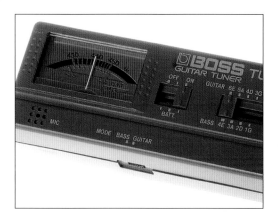

Electronic and digital tuners

Using an electronic or digital tuner is probably the easiest way to tune your guitar. This is especially true when you are a beginner, as you won't have to listen out for correct tuning, something which can take time to master.

There are quite a few electronic tuners to choose from, but they all work in a similar manner. You select which string you want to tune on the tuner, pluck the corresponding open string, and adjust the machine head until the needle or light settles on a zero or 440Hz mark. Electric guitars connect to the tuner with a lead but there is usually a small microphone on the tuner to pick up the sound from acoustic guitars. It's best to use a tuner in quiet surroundings to ensure your guitar is tuned accurately.

The main drawback with most electronic tuners is that you have to get the string close to perfect tuning before the display reacts and begins to show whether the tuning is too high or low. This can be frustrating when you first start out, as you have no point of reference or experience of the correct pitch. Try to avoid making the strings tune too high as this will overstretch the strings and may cause them to break. Always try to tune up to the correct pitch by making sure that the string is tuned too low to begin with. Unwinding the string a little before you start tuning can do this.

Tuners are available that will recognize any note on the guitar and let you tune it. These are called chromatic tuners and are slightly more expensive. The best of these tuners will track every note you play, giving you instant feedback on your tuning. The advantage of using these when you first start out is that, because they respond to any note, they tell you which note you are currently closest to and will make it easier to decide whether you need to tighten the string to make the note higher or loosen the string to lower the note.

Left: An electronic tuner

Pitch pipes

Tuning forks

Pitch pipes were used a lot before electronic tuners became cheaper and more reliable. They are similar to pan pipes and have six pipes to blow through, one for each string. You need to use your ears to match the tones produced from the pipes, and this takes practice.The tone produced by blowing into the pipes may vary slightly depending on how hard you blow. Any damage to the pipes will also affect the tones.

Tuning forks are another method of tuning by ear. You usually have a single tuning fork to which you tune one string and then tune the other strings from that one. Tuning forks are usually tuned to the A string at 440Hz but E-string tuning forks are also available.

Tuning to keyboards

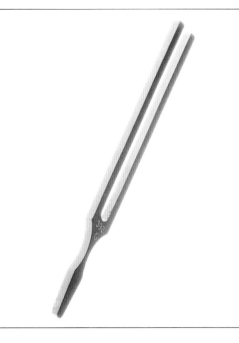

Another method for tuning by ear is to tune by using a keyboard. If you are playing in a band and tuning by ear, everyone should tune to the same instrument and electronic keyboards are best for this.

Right: A tuning fork
Far Right: Electronic keyboards can be used for tuning

You can tune either a single string to a keyboard and then tune the other strings to that one or you can tune each string to its relevant note on the keyboard. The second method is fine for electronic keyboards as you can usually rely on the tuning. But tuning to pianos can be problematic if the piano itself is not in tune.

The notes of the guitar

Before you can tune the guitar you need to know a few things about the notes and strings on a standard guitar.

The strings themselves are numbered from one through six with the top (thinnest) string numbered one. When strung on the guitar, each open string has a letter associated with it as well. This is the note it should be tuned to. The notes of a standard six-string guitar are:

E	A	D	G	B	E
6th	5th	4th	3rd	2nd	1st

The 6th E is the thickest string and the 1st E is the thinnest. Although both strings are E-notes, the thin one is two octaves higher in pitch than the thick one.

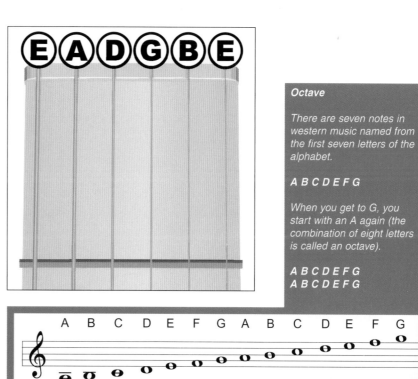

Octave

There are seven notes in western music named from the first seven letters of the alphabet.

A B C D E F G

When you get to G, you start with an A again (the combination of eight letters is called an octave).

A B C D E F G
A B C D E F G

The second occurrence of each letter is perfectly in tune with the first but is one octave higher in pitch. A standard piano has a keyboard that is seven and a quarter octaves from end to end.

It is usually helpful when first learning the notes on the guitar to make up a mnemonic to help remember them. Something like "Elvis And Dylan Got Big Egos" works quite well, with Elvis being the largest string. Knowing the names of the strings is enough to be able to tune using an electronic tuner, pitch pipes, and a keyboard.

With keyboards you need to be able to find the right note to tune to and then use your hearing to judge how close you are to it.

Here is a diagram that shows where the same notes lie on guitars and keyboards.

Tuning by ear can be difficult and how quickly you pick it up depends on what kind of ear you have for music.

Matching the notes of another instrument, whether a keyboard or pitch pipes, can be tricky because, even if the notes are the same, the sound of the instruments is quite different. You have to concentrate on listening to the pitch of that note, how high or low it sounds, and try to match it, ignoring the characteristics of the instrument.

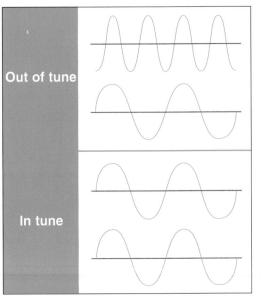

When tuning to electronic tuners, you should have the volume and tone controls of the guitar turned almost all the way up. Strike the string to be tuned once and watch the display while slowly tightening the string with the machine head. Let the plucked open string vibrate a while until the note starts to fade and then strike the string again. When you have achieved the correct tuning, the display should be steady on the optimum tuning mark and not swinging at all.

When a note holds a tone for a length of time it is referred to as "sustain."

Right: When the string is in tune the needle is steady in the center of the display

When you start getting close you can hear the two tones oscillate.

You want to be able to slow the oscillation down. If it speeds up again you have passed through the point of perfect tuning and you need to turn the machine heads in the opposite direction. Perfect tuning is achieved when the oscillation slows down and the two tones are perfectly matched.

If you are using a tuning fork to tune your guitar, hold the fork toward the bottom, where the two prongs join, with your thumb and forefinger. Strike the top of the fork once on the side of a chair or table and then hold the end of it against the body of the guitar to hear the tone.

It can be rather difficult holding the tuning fork, playing the string, and turning the machine heads all at the same time, so it is best to strike the string first and then the tuning fork with the same hand. If you manage to achieve this, you wil be listening for the same kind of oscillating effect that was described earlier, in which the difference between the two tones is reduced when oscillation slows right down. You should then be in tune.

You can only tune one string to the tuning fork. Which string this is depends on the pitch of the fork. Usually this is an A.

To tune one string to another, you need to know some of the notes on the fretboard and their relationship to each other. Look at the notes on the first five frets of the guitar. Whole notes such as these are referred to as being "natural notes."

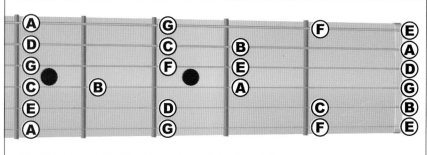

Left: Hold the tuning fork against the body of the guitar to hear it

If you look at the names of the open strings and compare them to the note names on the 5th fret one string down in tone, you will see that they are almost all the same. The only string that doesn't follow this pattern is the B string. The B appears on the fourth fret of the string below instead (see diagram on previous page).

These are all exactly the same note. The D on the 5th fret of the A string is exactly the same as the open D string. The same note, same pitch, same octave, same everything—it's a duplicate. Knowing this makes it possible to tune the guitar by comparing one open string to a fretted note on another string. To tune one string to another, follow the pattern in the diagram.

Right: Gently touch the string to play a harmonic

Tuning this way is a little easier as the notes should sound exactly the same. You should still be listening out for the oscillations in the tone.

Playing harmonics

You can use harmonics to help check your tuning, especially for the fine-tuning when you get very close. Harmonics are special tones that appear at certain points on the fretboard and can create a note without your having to press the string down onto the fret.

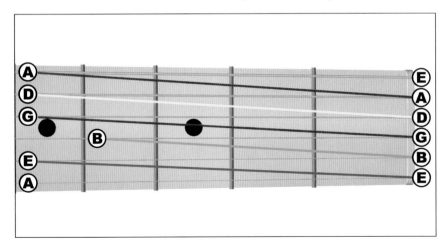

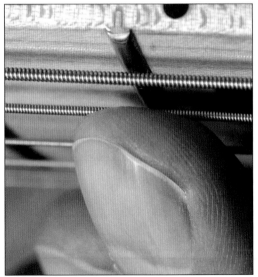

Harmonics appear at points along the length of the neck between the nut and bridge and fall on certain frets.

Harmonics fall on the 5th, 7th, 12th, 19th, and 24th fret (if you have one). The 24th fret position usually falls around the point where the front pickup is placed.

The 12th fret is halfway along the length of the string. The 5th and 24th frets are at one quarter and three-quarters of the way along the length, and the 7th and 19th frets are at one third and two-thirds.

To play a harmonic, lightly place your finger on the string above the correct fret without pushing down on it and pluck the string with a plectrum. You should hear a pure ringing tone.

You may have to vary the position of your finger over the fret slightly to get the best tone. Varying the position of where you strike the string with the plectrum also helps.

The harmonic position of the 12th fret is known as the first harmonic.
The harmonic position of the 7th fret is known as the second harmonic.
The harmonic position of the 5th fret is known as the third harmonic.

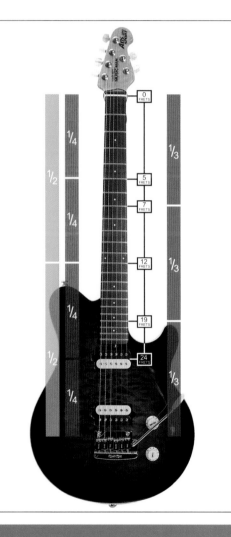

Left: A diagram showing the divisions of a string where harmonics appear

Alternative tunings

Harmonic tuning follows a similar pattern to tuning between strings. When playing harmonics, notice that the tones produced by the third harmonic are the same as the ones produced on the second harmonic of the next string up in pitch.

So this method can be used to tune or check tuning for all the strings except that awkward B string. It is best to use the string-to-string method for that one.

There are other tuning methods besides E A D G B E but this is the standard and most common form and the one that you will need to use to follow this book.

One popular variation of standard tuning is the "dropped D," where the bottom E string is detuned down to a D allowing for lower notes to be played. The open strings are then D A D G B E.

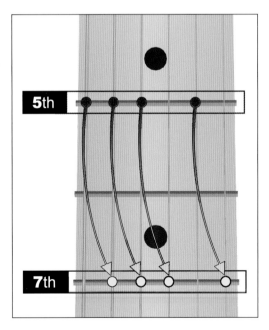

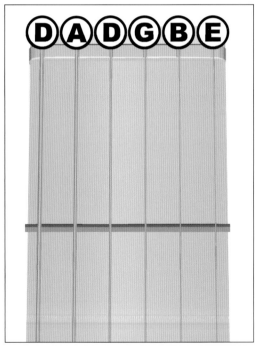

Sometimes people tune their guitars to a chord, so that when they play all the open strings it is already playing a full chord.

Tuning to the E major or E minor chord is quite common, allowing for chords to be formed by placing the finger flat across all the strings. Tuning to D or G are other alternatives used.

These methods are sometimes used in blues and country music, where the guitars are often played with slides or bottlenecks.

Note that detuning strings down to notes lower than how they were meant to sound can cause buzzing of strings against frets, as the string is slacker than before.

Retuning guitars can also affect the neck, as most guitars are set up for standard tuning with careful adjustment of the truss rod. The different string tensions used in alternative tuning methods may twist the neck of your guitar.

Alternative tuning methods also require you to learn new note positions and the chord shapes to fit them.

Left: Various bottlenecks and slides

Basic Playing Skills

This chapter begins by looking at what chords are and how they are formed.

As chords are often difficult to form with your fingers when you first learn to play, let's begin with some simple and partial chords that can be formed with only a few strings and a couple of fingers.

Once the left-hand fingers get to grips with the chord shapes we'll explain the principles of rhythm.

When first starting to play, it can take time getting the muscles in your fingers to form the shapes required of them, so take as long as you need before moving on.

When your fingers are ready, you can begin to form full chords. We'll start by looking at a few of the most common ones.

Playing position

Before embarking on your first few chords we should look at the position you are going to adopt while playing the guitar.

It doesn't really matter whether you sit or stand when playing the guitar but, if you are standing for long periods of time with a heavy guitar strapped around your neck and shoulders, you will begin to feel the strain.

It makes sense to sit and play while working things out and then stand if rehearsing for performance to build up your stamina.

Whatever your choice, comfort is the main objective. You should not have to hold your guitar up with your hands, it should either be hanging correctly from the strap or resting on your legs if sitting. Your hands must be free to play and not take the weight of the guitar.

Far Right: Standing to play guitar
Right: Sitting to play guitar

It is usual to sit on a stool to play, as the arms of a chair will restrict your movement. The height you sit at is not important and it doesn't matter which leg you use to rest the guitar on or whether your legs are crossed. The length of the strap is equally unimportant as long as it's comfortable.

Your left hand should be able to move comfortably along the whole length of the neck of the guitar without putting any strain on your wrist. Try placing the pad of your thumb against the center of the back of the guitar neck and lay the fingers of the same hand across the strings, then run your hand up and down the neck a few times to check.

The position of the left hand partly depends on the size of your hands and whether you like the top of the guitar to be high or low. Whatever position you choose you should be able to move your thumb quickly and easily from the center to the edge of the neck.

Your right hand should be free to stroke all the strings evenly with the pick or plectrum and move between both pickups or across the hole while strumming.

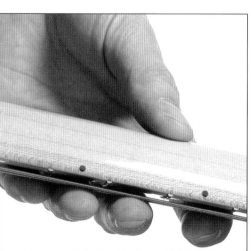

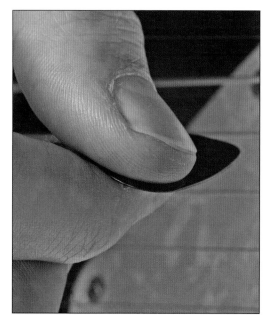

Far Left: Place the thumb against the center of the neck
Left: Hold the plectrum between thumb and forefinger

When strumming the guitar, most of the movement should come from the wrist. Your arm should be relaxed and a small amount of movement will come from the forearm.

The plectrum is held between the thumb and first finger but don't grip it too tightly as this will tense your hand. It takes a while to find the right balance between grip and relaxation and a few plectrums are likely to go flying across the room until you find your balance.

When first learning to play, there is always the tendency to tense up and start gripping the guitar and plectrum—try taking regular breaks and force yourself to relax. You will have better

control and reflexes if you are relaxed. Even when you see your idols thrashing and throwing the guitar around with angst and fury, they are controlled in their playing. So, relax and enjoy yourself.

The position you adopt for playing your guitar will also depend on the style of guitar and music that you choose. Lead guitarists tend to concentrate the playing area toward the body of the guitar, while rhythm guitarists favor creating shapes toward the end of the guitar.

Right: Nails should be short and clean

Left-handed players

Your hands and nails should be clean and dry and any chips or splits in your nails should be filed out so that the rough edges don't catch on the strings.

Your left-hand nails should be cut short, as long nails make it difficult to hold the strings against the frets. Right-hand nails can be longer if you want to use them to pick at the strings but they can easily catch and tear on the strings while strumming if you are not careful.

Left-handers adopt different solutions for playing the guitar.

Some people just turn a right-handed guitar upside down and work out ways of playing everything back-to-front and upside down! Others string the guitar in reverse, as well as turning the guitar around to keep the thicker strings to the top. This can affect the neck and make it twist, as thicker strings create more tension on the neck than thin ones and the truss rod will have been set up for a right-handed player.

Special left-handed guitars are easier to find these days so you shouldn't have to adapt a right-handed one. Other left-handers just play right-handed. The text and diagrams in this book assume you will be learning to play right-handed, so you'll have to make the necessary adjustments if you want to play any other way.

Left: A variety of left-handed guitars

Exercising

Chords

Unfortunately, there is no escaping from pain. When you first start playing the guitar it will be painful and not just for your ears! The tips of the fingers on your left hand are likely to become sore and blistered and the muscles of the fingers may become stiff.

However, in a short time, the skin will toughen and your muscles will get used to the different positions so that you shouldn't feel too much pain. If you stop playing for a significant amount of time, you may find these problems will reoccur.

If you are experiencing problems at this stage, don't give up, but try resting the hands on alternate days rather than continuing to practice.

As with any physical work, it is a good idea to warm up the muscles before starting and relax them again after playing. You can do this by flexing the fingers repeatedly, gently stretching the wrist and fingers back and forth with the other hand and shaking out the hands and fingers afterward.

You can regularly exercise the fingers by drumming them back and forth rhythmically. You can also buy finger exercisers from guitar stores. Squeezing a soft ball repeatedly also helps.

Before you attempt some simple chords, you'll need to understand what chords and notes are.

Chords are groups of notes that sound good together, having tones that complement each other. Fortunately, there are rules that can be applied to these relationships between the notes that help make remembering and working out chords easier.

There are seven notes in western music, labeled A through G, and chords are named after these notes. The chord of G will have the G note as its main or "root" note. The rest of the notes in the chord are those that fall at specific places within the root note's scale.

A scale is a set pattern of notes also based on the root note that informs you of all the possible harmonious notes that can be played alongside the root note.

G major chord

Let's have a closer look at this by using the G note as our root note. The scale of G major is made up of the notes G, A, B, C, D, E and F sharp. The reasons why will be explained later. The G major chord is made up of three notes called a "triad"; these notes are the 1st, 3rd and 5th notes of the scale. In this case the G, B and D notes.

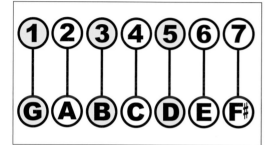

If you know the notes of a major scale you can easily work out the major chord, as it is always the 1st, 3rd and 5th notes.

You can easily play a G major chord on a guitar by strumming the three open strings D, G and B and making sure you avoid or block the other three strings. Unfortunately not all chords are this easy.

Left: Open string G major.

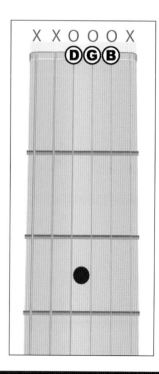

When using your fingers on the fretboard to obtain a note, or fretting a note, hold the string behind the fret, towards the headstock, and not on the fret itself. To give a good clean tone, the string needs to be able to resonate freely from the fret up to the bridge. You are, in effect, shortening the string to change its tuning. If you place your finger directly on the fret you dampen or deaden the sound.

On a keyboard you can get away with just playing three note chords but a guitar has six strings that need to be played. We need to find a way to include more strings in the chord. We can enhance the sound of the chord by adding some extra 1st, 3rd and 5th notes to it, in this case some extra G, B or D notes.

If you look again at all the notes at the bottom end of the fretboard you can see that by holding down the thin top E string at the 3rd fret, it would be easy to add another G note to the chord. This actually makes the chord easier to play, as you only have to avoid playing the two thick bottom strings, the E and the A. This gives the chord a high thin sound but emphasizes the G as it includes two of them.

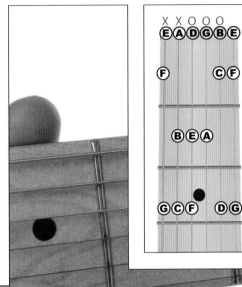

Right: One finger G major on top E

To give the chord a deeper tone we could add a note from one of the thicker strings instead. There is a B note on the 2nd fret of the A string. Place your finger at this fret and play the chord, avoiding both the E strings.

We can extend this chord further by adding the G note that lies on the bottom E string. This is at the 3rd fret as it was for the top E. Place your index finger on the 2nd fret of the A string and your second finger on the 3rd fret of the bottom E string.

To play the G chord, start by picking the notes one by one to make sure that they all sound clear and none are being blocked by your fingers, then start to strum them faster until it sounds as though all the strings are playing as one tone.

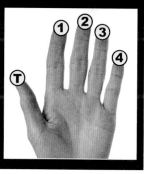

Numbering the fingers

Our chord diagrams will now all be labeled with numbers that represent the four fingers of the left hand; a "T" will be used if we need to use the thumb.

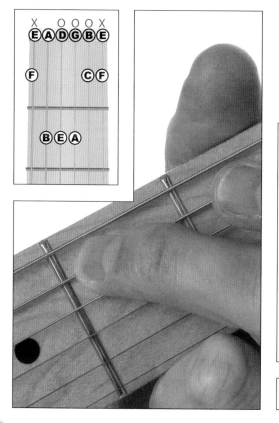

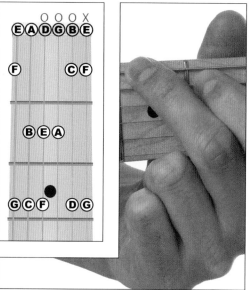

Far Left: One finger G major on A string
Left: Two finger G major

Right & Far Right: Full G major chords

Try playing the chord in different ways with your right hand. You can play it slowly or quickly, firmly or softly, from the front of the body or towards the bridge at the rear of the body. Listen to the different sounds produced when playing the same chord in different ways.

The full G major chord, utilizing all six strings uses the G note from the top E as well as B and G. You can add the third finger to the top E string at the 3rd fret to play this chord. You may find this stretch difficult at first but keep practicing and it will become easier.

An alternative way of forming this chord is by using the second, third and fourth fingers instead. You may have difficulty using the little finger at this stage of your development but using these fingers leaves your hand better positioned for playing other chords.

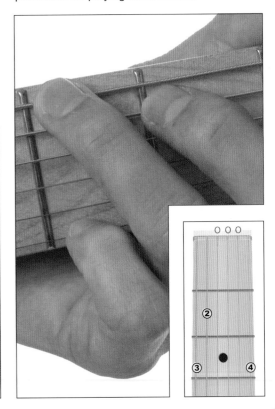

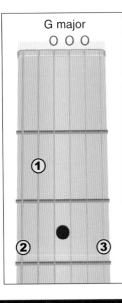

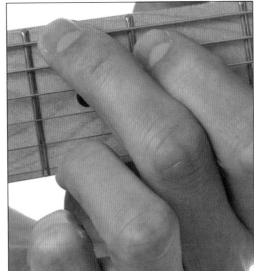

As you can see, in order to create chords you have to find the correct notes on the fretboard and then place your fingers at these points. Looking at the fretboard diagram you can see that there are a number of places where the notes G, B and D appear and you can make a G major chord by fretting at any of these points.

Although all of these chords are made up of the same notes, they sound slightly different from each other. This is because they have different balances of notes to them. One may have more Gs than Bs or Ds while another may have more Bs. These different forms of the same chord are referred to as inversions.

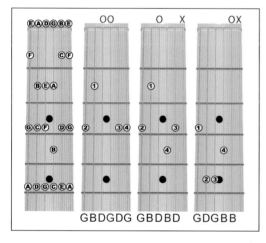

GBDGDG GBDBD GDGBB

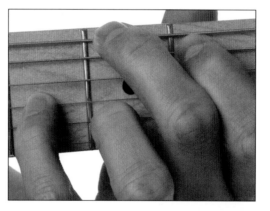

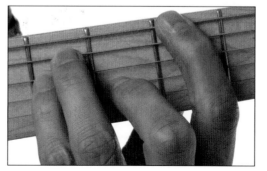

Far Left, Top Left & Left:
Alternative G major chords

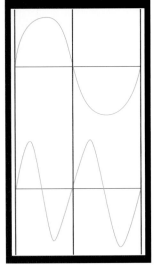

If we could see the waveforms that each of the tones makes we would see that each octave up would have a waveform that is exactly half the length of the lower one.

Right: Each repetition of a scale rises or lowers in pitch

Another factor affecting the sound of the chord is the balance between low notes and high notes. If you look at the original G major chord you can see that there are three G notes in it. If you play each G in turn you will hear that, although they are the same note, they have different tones or pitches. This is because when you get to the end of the seven notes in a scale they start again, repeating and rising in pitch. The second G is eight notes, an octave, away from the first G. Each repetition of a note is either an octave higher or lower than the other in pitch.

The main thing to remember with major chords is that they are made up of the 1st, 3rd, and 5th notes of their scale and we can play as many or as few of these notes as we want and they will still make the correct sound of the chord. This is useful to know when first learning to play when your fingers won't stretch enough to create the full chord. You can pick and choose which notes to play to make partial chords. Just remember to ignore or deaden any strings that have notes that don't fall within the chord.

C major chord

Let's expand our repertoire and look at another partial chord that we can play.

The next chord we will tackle is the C major chord. This time we will be using the 1st, 3rd, and 5th notes from the C scale. Scales will be explained in depth in Chapter Four.

The scale of C major is C, D, E, F, G, A, B which means that the C major chord is made up of C, E, and G. If you look at the notes on the fret board you can work out where the notes of the chord can fall.

A two finger version is available using the bottom four strings and ignoring the top two.

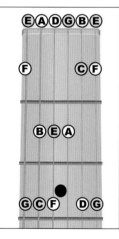

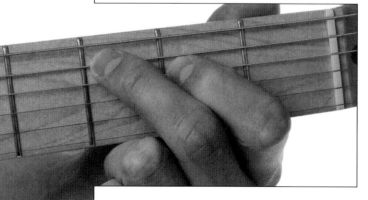

At its simplest, C major can be played with one finger placed on the 1st fret of the B string, ignoring the bottom three strings.

Try both of these, once again picking through the strings one by one to make sure that they all sound clear before strumming through them as a chord.

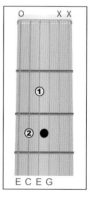

Top Left: One finger C major
Bottom Left: Two finger C major

Chord changes

Now that you have two chords to play, you should start to practice changing between them. At first, this will be a slow process as your fingers struggle to form the shapes, but eventually changing chords should become second nature to you.

Use the two finger versions of the chords to practice the chord changes and try using your second and third fingers as well as your first and second.

Start by counting four downward strokes of the G major chord and then change to the C major for a count of four. Try to keep the timing slow and even and avoid long pauses between the chord changes. Remember not to press down too hard on the frets, you should use just enough pressure to get the strings to touch the fretboard. A light touch allows for quicker changes.

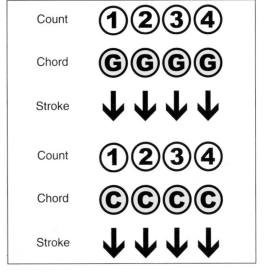

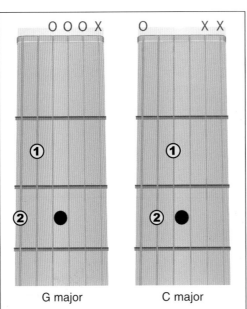

Right: Two finger G and C major chords

G major   C major

When you have a good steady count of four with your downward strokes, start adding upward strokes with the plectrum between some of the counts, still playing the downward strokes at the same speed as before.

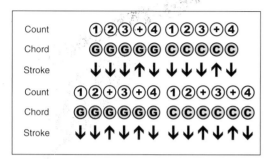

When you feel confident playing around with these chords, try to add some variety by changing chords on the two as well as on the four. Also try to vary the rhythm by adding extra strokes between each count, building up to three or four strokes for each count.

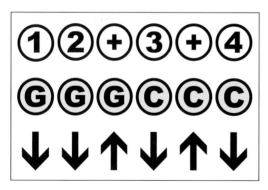

When you feel you can change between chords confidently, try to change chords for just one count.

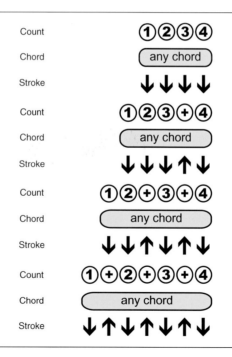

Practice playing rhythms by following exercise patterns such as this one.

Out for the count

Most popular music is in four-four time, which means that there are four beats to the bar. When music is written, it is split into sections of equal time that are known as bars. As far as we are concerned at the moment this means that the music is counted out in fours.

1 2 3 4 1 2 3 4.

If you are counting the spaces between the counts you should use the word "and" without varying the timing of the numbers.

1 + 2 + 3 + 4.

Sharps and flats

The two chords we have already looked at work well together but a third chord would give some variety to the sound and add another level of complexity for the fingers to cope with.

The third chord we will look at is D major. The major scale for D is D, E, F#, G, A, B, C#, so the 1st, 3rd, and 5th notes are D, F# and A.

This is the first time we have had to play a sharp note so we should have a closer look at what sharp notes are before playing the chord.

If you look at the notes of the fretboard you will notice that there are spaces between some of the notes. If there is a space between two notes the space will be either a sharp or flat note. This means that the second fret of the bottom E string, between the F and G notes, will be either an F sharp or a G flat note. Notes are called sharp as they rise to the next note and flat as they fall to the one below.

F sharp and G flat, for example, are regarded as being the same note, the two notes are known as "enharmonic equivalents".

These sharps and flats on the guitar neck are the same as the black notes on a keyboard.

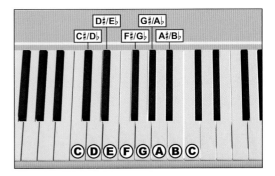

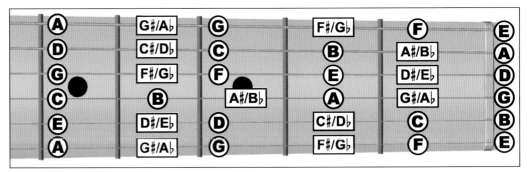

Right: All the notes of the first five frets including sharps and flats

You may have noticed that there is no gap between the B and C notes and the E and F notes. This is because B sharp is the same as a C note and C flat is the same as B. The same applies to the E and F notes. If you look at a keyboard you will see that there are no black notes between B and C or E and F.

To help you work out whether to call a note by its sharp or flat name, there is a general rule to follow that states that no note should appear twice in a scale. This means that in a scale you cannot have both a C note and a C sharp note, you would have to call the C sharp a D flat instead. So in the scale for G major you have to use an F sharp because the G is already present in the scale.

There are musical symbols that represent sharps and flats.

The symbol for sharp is #

The symbol for flat is ♭

If a note is neither sharp nor flat it is said to be natural and the symbol for a natural note is ♮

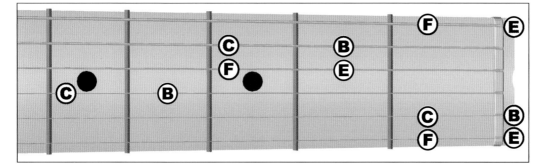

Left: There is no space for sharp or flat notes between these notes

D major chord

Returning to the D major chord, we now need to identify where the notes of this chord, D, F sharp, and A, lie along the fretboard.

If we stick to the bottom four strings that we have been using with the G and C major chords, we can create a D major chord by placing one finger on the 2nd fret of the bottom E and another on the 2nd fret of the G string.

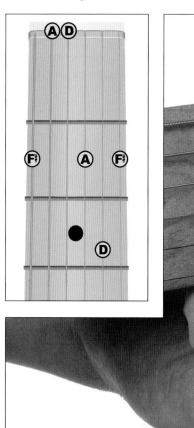

Top Right: Occurrences of A, D, and F#
Right: Two finger D major chord

Again, you should make sure that you can hear all the notes cleanly before strumming the chord, then try changing between all three chords.

repeated patterns know as "riffs." Now you have your first tune, based around the G major chord.

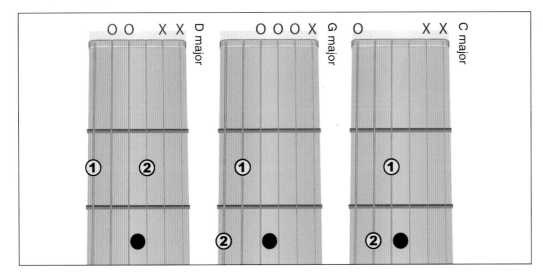

When you can play the above pattern comfortably, try changing the chords every two counts. Play around with the rhythm, order, and timing of these chords to build tunes or short

Notice how the sound of the tune seems to want to return to the G major chord at the end of the run. The tune is said to be in the key of G major. We'll look at keys in depth in Chapter Four.

A grouping of three chords such as the one you have just been using is known as a "three-chord trick" and many songs have been written around them. There is a three-chord trick for every key, as we shall see later.

Left: Two finger versions of G, C, and D chords

Full chords

Top Right: G major chord using second, third, and fourth fingers
Bottom Far Right: G major chord using first, second, and third fingers
Bottom Right: C major chord

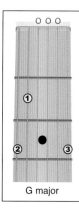

G major

G major

As your fingers become comfortable forming these two finger chords you should start to replace them with full six-string chords. All of the chords covered so far use three fingers when they are played correctly but you may find some of them a bit of a stretch at first.

The G major chord requires the widest stretch, as you will need to reach the G note on both the top and bottom E strings. Try to do this using your first, second, and third fingers and then using your second, third, and fourth fingers to see which you find more comfortable.

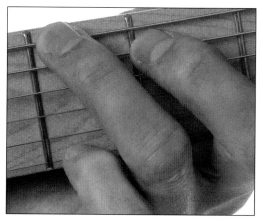

The C major chord is a little easier to form. Place your first finger on the 1st fret of the B string to make a C and then place your second and third fingers in the same place as before.

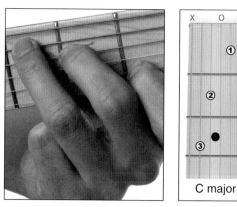

C major

The D major chord is quite simple to form but can be tricky when moving from one of the other chords we have covered.

Place your first finger on the 2nd fret of the G string to make an A note. Next place your second finger on the 2nd fret of the top E string to make a G and then place your third finger on the 3rd fret of the B string which makes a D.

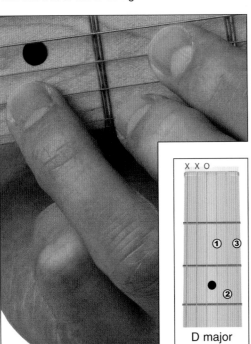

D major

Alternatively, you could lay the first finger across all three top strings and use your second or third finger for the D note. This is called barring the frets.

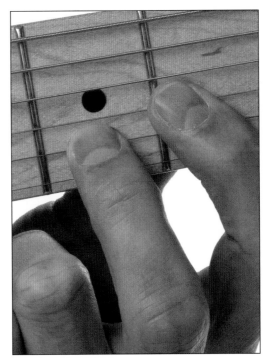

These full chords sound much richer in tone than the partial versions, but you should feel free to experiment with them all to give you the sound you want from the music.

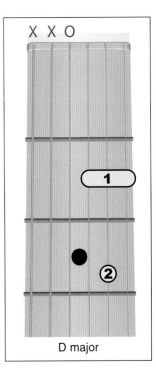

X X O

D major

Far Left: D major chord
Left: D major bar

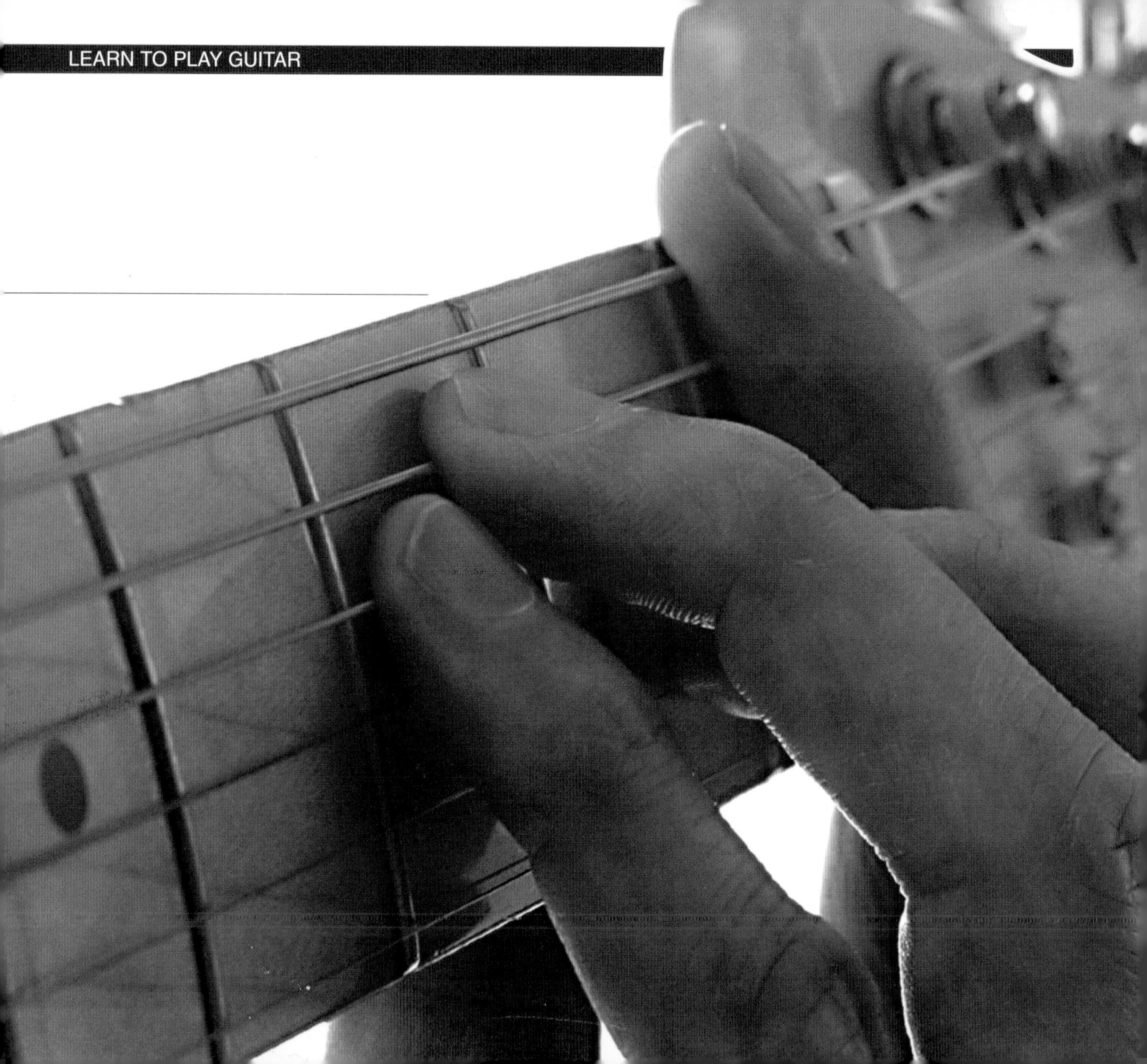

The Bar Chord

In this chapter we will start to look at bar or barre chords. Bar chords are those which do not use open strings and are so-called because the guitarist uses one finger, usually the index finger, to form a bar across the strings on the fretboard.

The main shape of this type of chord is based on the F major chord and the fingers can be moved up and down the guitar neck holding this shape, stopping at any note on the bottom E string, to play the major chord of that note. We'll also look at the minor version of this chord, as well as how to play major and minor bar chords on the A string. This will greatly expand the number of chords that you can play with only small changes to the overall chord shape.

Although the chord shape may seem a little difficult to get used to at first, it is an important one to learn as it will allow you to play many chords, simply by learning the notes that are placed along the length of the neck.

Forming the chord

The bar chord was used almost exclusively by punk bands in the Seventies and is still the favored version of chord-playing for many rock bands. Because of the power of the sound, using all six strings and the speed with which you can change from one chord to the next, this chord is extremely well suited to the thin necks of electric guitars.

This chord uses all four fingers and all six strings but, as previously suggested, you can leave out notes in order to play partial chords if you wish. To do this, either don't play the string you want to leave out with the right hand or make use of a finger on the left hand to block the note.

To create the bar chord, you need to place your index finger across all the strings. We'll place this bar three frets up the neck where the first dot is on the fretboard. This will create a G major chord when complete.

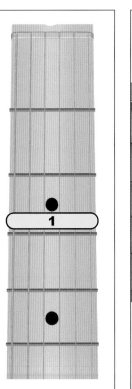

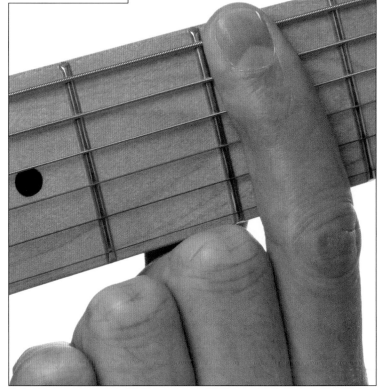

Right: Barring across the string with the index finger

When barring the neck, the index finger should be placed behind the fret and as close to it as possible without being directly on top of it. Try not to press down too hard on the strings. The less pressure you can exert on the neck, the quicker you'll be able to change to another chord. The amount of pressure needed will vary between guitars, depending on how high the action is. Placing your thumb toward the center of the back of the guitar neck may help you maintain correct and even pressure.

With your index finger barred across the strings, try picking the strings one by one with the right hand to check that the note is playing correctly and not buzzing on the fret. If you hear buzzing, try adjusting your finger position slightly. If you still get a lot of buzzing, relax and try again. This technique usually takes some time to perfect. You should aim to achieve a flat surface across the strings with your index finger, which may require you to rotate the position of the hand slightly, and use the outer edge of the finger for barring. With practice, the correct positioning of the index finger will come naturally.

If you find this finger position too uncomfortable, you can try the "thumb-over" method described later in this chapter.

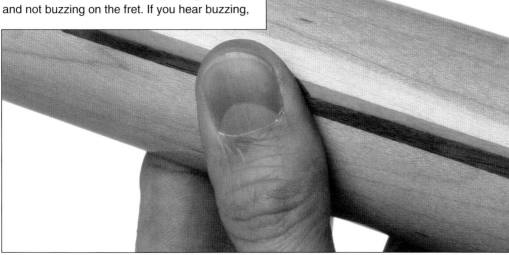

Left: Placing the thumb near the center of the neck may help with finger placement

The Bottom is the top

Remember that the bottom E string is actually the top of the six strings when looking at the guitar neck. It is called "bottom E" because it has the lowest tone, not because of its physical position.

Right: The full major bar chord for the bottom E string

Don't worry at first if the center strings, A, D, and G, do not sound right, because we'll be adding notes to these strings using other fingers. The main aim is to get good clean notes from the bottom E and top E strings.

Once you are comfortable with the placement of the index finger, you can add the second, third, and fourth fingers.

Place your second finger one fret up from the index finger on the G string.

Place your third finger on the A string at the 5th fret. Place your fourth finger just below your third finger, on the same fret but on the D string. This may feel slightly awkward at first, but, again, with practice it will become easier.

Try not to press too hard on the strings. Pick out the notes one by one and adjust your positioning until they all sound clean. You will probably need to rest occasionally and come back to this point. Relax your hands and stretch the fingers between sessions.

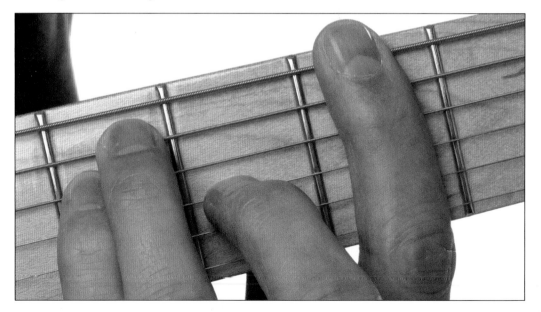

The thumb-over method

A bar chord can also be formed by using your thumb over the top of the neck of the guitar and pressing down on the bottom E string instead of barring all the way across the strings with your index finger. Use your index finger to bar just the top B and E strings. You need to use the knuckle area of the thumb to grip the string. Alternatively, you could ignore the bottom E and just play the other five strings, which can sometimes give a lighter sound to the bar chord.

You may have to lower the position that you use to hold the neck of the guitar to achieve this method of playing.

Left: Using the thumb to hold down the bottom E string

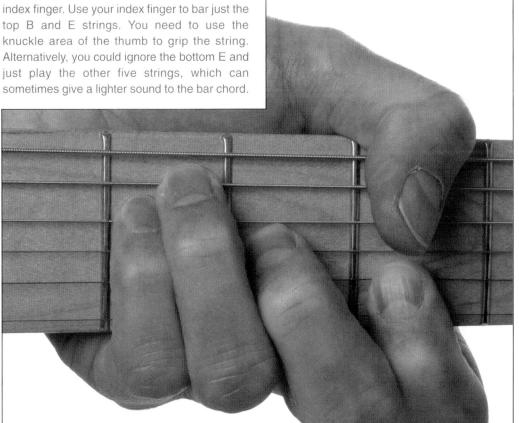

Playing and moving the bar chord

Right: Moving the bar chord

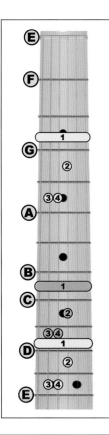

When you begin to feel comfortable with the finger position, try relaxing the grip so that your fingers are lying just on top of the strings. Practice gripping and relaxing the strings with your fingers on the fretboard while strumming the strings with the right hand from top to bottom. When your fingers are relaxed you should notice that the chord sounds short and choppy. That is because relaxing the grip shortens and deadens the notes.

You can develop this method by playing a fast rhythm with the right hand, occasionally pressing the fingers of your left hand down onto the fretboard to "sound" the chord. You can easily create a reggae-type sound using this technique.

Once you are comfortable forming this chord, you should start trying to slide it to other positions along the neck. This changes the name of the chord to the note that you stop at on the E string. If you want to play a G major chord, slide your finger forming the bar to the 3rd fret. C major is at the 8th fret and D major is at the 10th fret.

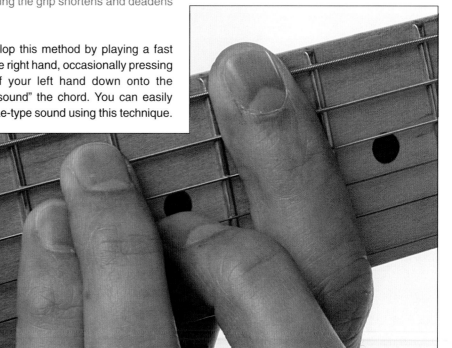

Partial bar chords

If you are having trouble forming or moving the bar chord, you can still play partial chords.

One option is to play just the bottom three strings, which will create a heavy-sounding chord. This can be played with either two or three fingers depending on what you can manage.

For a lighter-sounding version of the bar chord you can play just the top three or four strings of it, which is almost the same as using the thumb-over method.

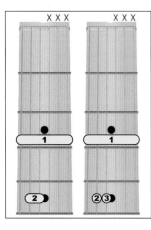

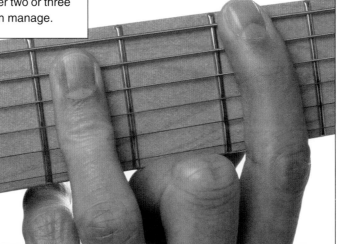

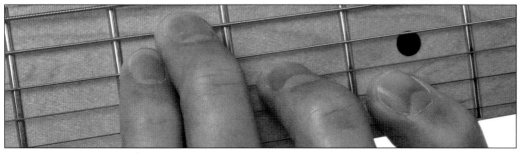

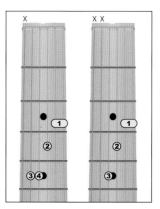

Top Left: A bar chord created using just two fingers

Bottom Left: Major bar chord ignoring bottom E string

Moving to the A string

It is quite a long distance to slide the bar chord between the G and D positions along the bottom E string. This can be difficult if a quick chord change is needed.

Fortunately there is a solution—you can also play a bar chord on the A string. This chord is similar to the one used on the bottom E string and in some respects it is even easier to form.

The chord is based on the B major chord shape. Because the chord is being played along the A string, you have to ignore the bottom E string, either by not playing it or by blocking it with one of your fingers so that it doesn't sound.

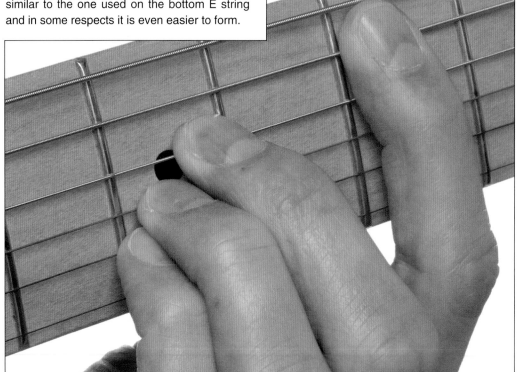

Right: Major bar chord for playing on the A string

Forming the chord

As with the last bar chord, you begin by barring the first finger across the strings. Do this across the 3rd fret again. This time don't include the bottom E, but you can use your finger to block it.

Place your second finger on the 5th fret of the D string, then your third finger on the 5th fret of the G string and your fourth finger on the 5th fret of the B string. Depending on the size of your fingers, they may feel a bit cramped together. You may have to place one finger slightly behind the other one but still between the frets. Check that the notes are sounding clearly by picking each string in turn.

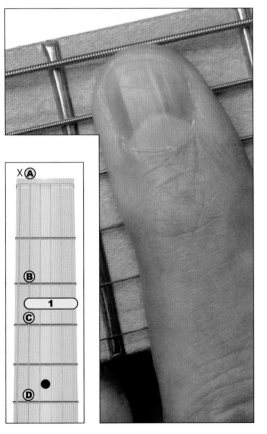

You have just created a C major chord using the A string. If you slide this chord shape up the neck by two frets you will have a D major chord. When you get used to forming and changing between the shapes of these chords, you will find this is a much quicker way to reach the C and D major chords from the G major on the E string.

Far Left: Index finger blocking the bottom E string

Left: C major bar chord on the 5th fret of a string

You may be able to make this chord just by using your index and third fingers, barring your third finger across the 5th frets of the D, G, and B strings. Try picking each string again to see if they all play correctly. If this method doesn't work, you can use it as a partial chord, ignoring the top E string.

You can now slide this chord up and down the neck to create chords for each note that lies along the A string.

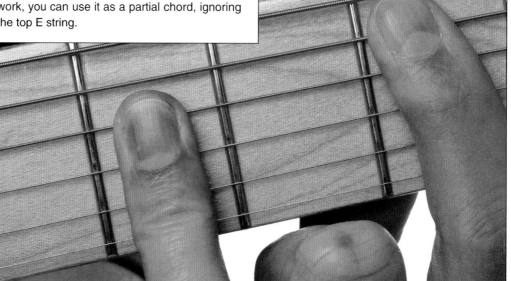

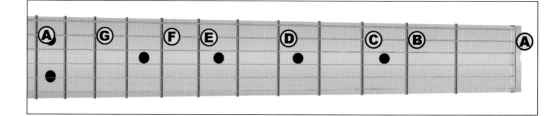

Right: Two finger version of the major bar chord for the A string

Beyond the 12th fret

So far we have only looked at notes that fall within the first twelve frets, as acoustic guitars do not have much reach beyond this point. However, electric guitars are designed to go much further.

As mentioned in the first chapter, the 12th fret has a double inlay half way along the length of the string. It produces a note one octave higher than its open string. This means that once you go beyond the 12th fret the pattern of notes repeats again from the open string. For example, the G note is three frets along from the E string, so its octave is three frets up from the 12th fret at the 15th fret. There are always 12 frets between notes with the same name.

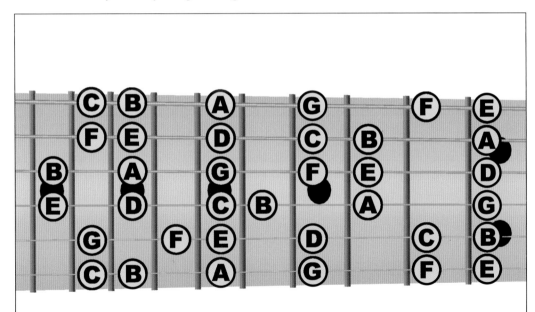

Minor chords

Using the major bar chords on both the E and A strings gives you nearly two octaves' worth of chords to play with, but there are other types of chord that have different sounds and give music different moods and feelings.

A minor chord takes only one small change from the major chord to form it. As we saw in the last chapter, a major chord is created from the 1st, 3rd, and 5th notes of a major scale. The minor chord is made up of the 1st, 3rd, and 5th notes of a minor scale.

There is another way of describing how to form a minor chord. This is done by flattening the 3rd note of the major chord. So, for example, if we look at the notes of a G major chord, the 1st note being G, the 3rd B, and the 5th D and we then flatten the third note, turning the B into a B flat, we create a G minor chord. In practice, you have to move the finger holding the 3rd note down one fret.

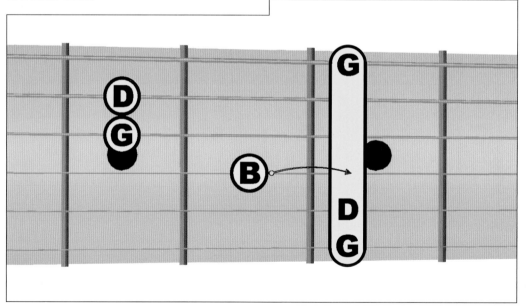

This is simple to do and makes the minor chords slightly easier to form. To play a minor bar chord on the E string, remove your second finger from the fretboard.

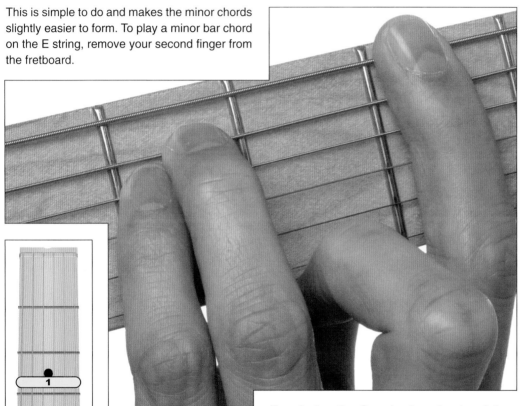

Try playing the G major bar chord and then removing and replacing your second finger to hear the difference between the two chords. Despite such a small change, the difference is noticeable, with the minor version sounding more dramatic.

Left: The minor bar chord for the bottom E string

To create a minor bar chord on the A string you still have to move the 3rd note back one fret. The third note falls where the fourth finger was placed for the major chord.

This creates a shape that is the same as a major chord on the E string. Again, you should ignore or block the bottom E string.

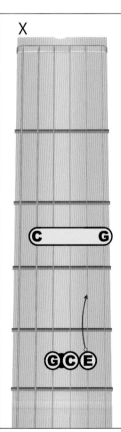

Right: The minor bar chord for the A string

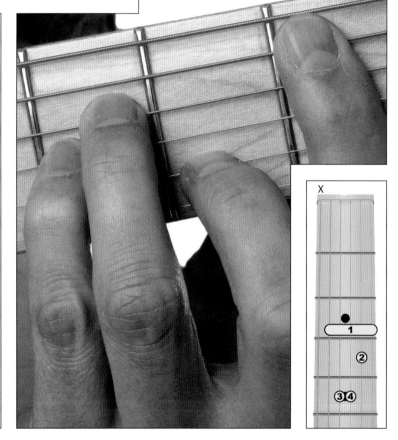

Alternative bar chords

The bar chord shapes we have covered so far are the most frequent, but there are others. We can look at a few alternatives that you can try.

There is a major bar chord for the top E string that is easier to play the closer you get to the top end of the neck. To create it, you have to bar your index finger across the top four strings and then place the fourth finger three frets up on the top E string. The bottom two strings are not played.

The name of the chord is taken from the note held down by the fourth finger on the top E string. So if you wanted to play a D major using this shape, you would bar the first finger across the 7th fret and place the fourth finger on the 10th fret of the top E string.

Left: An alternative major bar chord for the top E string

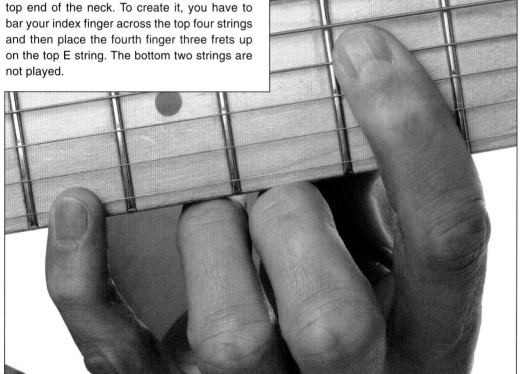

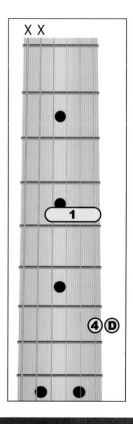

Right: An alternative major bar chord for the B string

You can play a major bar chord based on the notes that fall along the B string as well. To create this, you have to use your index finger to bar across the top three strings, then place your second finger one fret up on the B string and the third finger one fret further up on the D string. The name of the chord is taken from the note held by the second finger on the B string. Again, the bottom two strings are not played.

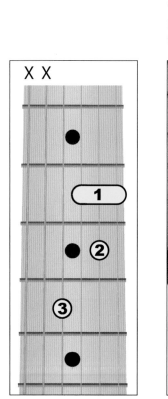

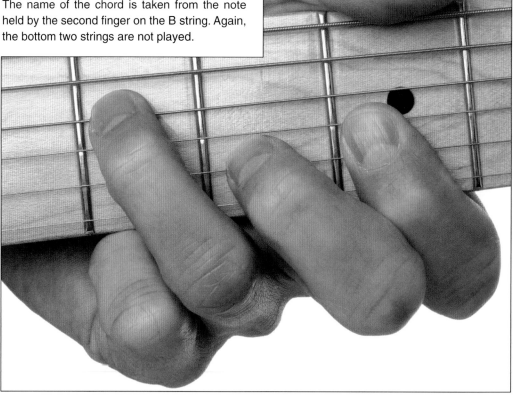

An alternative minor bar chord can be created based upon the notes of the B string. Place your index finger on the top E string, your second finger one fret up on the G string, your third finger one fret up on the D string, and your fourth finger on the same fret but on the B string. Don't play the bottom two strings. The name of the chord is taken from the note on the B string that is held by the fourth finger.

You will now have a large repertoire of chords to use, with only a few chord shapes to remember. Using partial chords and the alternative shapes will give even more variety to the sounds you can produce.

Practice forming and changing between chord shapes. We'll look at which chords work well together in the next chapter.

Left: An alternative minor bar chord for the B string

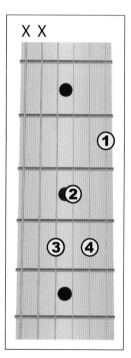

Major and Minor Keys

Now that you have some experience of playing a range of chords, we can look more closely at the relationships that exist between various chords. This will help you to construct songs.

We'll take a look at common groupings of chords for each key, giving you a range of three-chord tricks to practice and to use in songs.

We'll also look at the Circle of Fifths, a great tool for working out which chords work well together.

We'll finish the chapter by looking at how to add extra notes to extend the regular chords you have learned thus far.

Scales

We started to look at keys and scales in Chapter Two. We need to look at them in more detail, however, so that you can understand how scales are constructed and what uses they may have.

Keys and scales are intrinsically linked, in that the scale you play will depend upon which key you are in. The chords in that key are determined by the notes in the scale.

In order to get a better understanding of music and songwriting, the first thing to look at is the root note.

All songs have a root note and it is this note that helps to define the key and scale that the tune is in. Sometimes other instruments determine the key as some are tuned to certain keys or only have certain notes accessible to them. Sometimes singers are only able to sing in certain keys. In these cases the key that you play or write in is dictated by these limits, otherwise you are free to choose whatever note you want to base your tune around.

There are seven natural notes in western music plus five sharps or flats, making a total of twelve possible notes.

The full range of notes is:

A
A sharp or B flat (enharmonic equivalents)
B
C
C sharp or D flat (enharmonic equivalents)
D
D sharp or E flat (enharmonic equivalents)
E
F
F sharp or G flat (enharmonic equivalents)
G
G sharp or A flat (enharmonic equivalents)

The distance or interval between each of these notes is one half-step called a semitone.

A semitone is the distance between one fret and another.

A tone is equivalent to two semitones and so a tone is two frets along the fretboard.

You can base your tune around any one of these notes by forming a scale and key from it as well. A scale is a predictable pattern made from a selection of these notes starting from the root note. The key can be thought of as being the chords that are based on the notes in the scale.

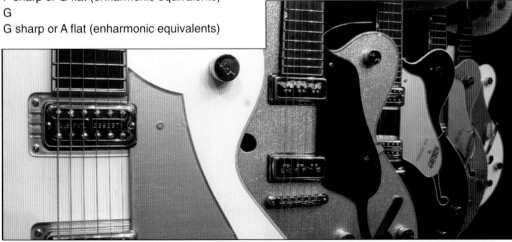

Major scales

If we start by looking at the major scales and keys we can see how this works in practice.

The notes in a major scale always follow this pattern; Tone, Tone, Semitone, Tone, Tone, Tone, Semitone

Remembering this pattern will help you pick seven of the twelve possible notes available to make a major scale.

The major scale is also known as the Ionian scale.

If we look at the notes that fall along the neck, we can see that the distance between F and G is two frets or a tone and the distance between B and C is one fret or a semitone.

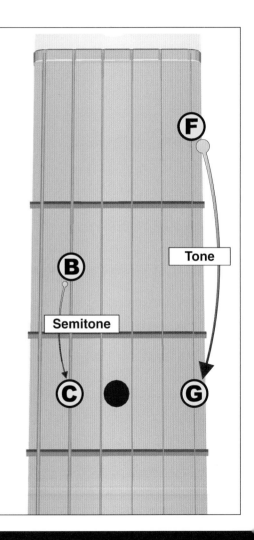

C major scale

To examine this major scale theory, we can look at the C major scale. This scale is made up of only the natural notes, so it has no sharp or flat notes in it. When it is played on a keyboard it uses only the white keys.

Using the TTSTTTS pattern and starting with the root note of C we can work out the other notes in the scale.

If we move two frets up from C we get to D.
Another tone up brings us to E.
A semitone or single fret up from E is F.
A tone up from F is G.
Another tone up lies A.
One more tone up is B.

Finally, a semitone up from B brings us back to C. So the C major scale is C D E F G A B and it has no sharp or flat notes in it.

As we have already learned, to create a major chord we use the 1st, 3rd, and 5th notes from the scale. So a C major chord is made up of C, E, and G.

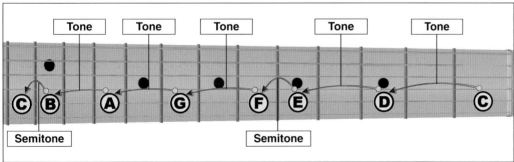

G major scale

Let's take a look at another example. This time it's the scale of G major.

We start with the root note of G.
One tone up from G is A.
Another tone up brings us to B.
A semitone up is C.
One tone up from C is D.
Another tone up is E.
The final tone brings us to F sharp or G flat.
And the final semitone returns us to G.

So, the scale for G major is G A B C D E F#. We call the final tone F sharp rather than G flat, because the general rule for scales is that no name of a note should appear more than once in the scale.

The G major chord is made up of the 1st, 3rd, and 5th notes of the G major scale making it G, B, and D.

With this knowledge you can make a scale and major chord for each of the twelve notes.

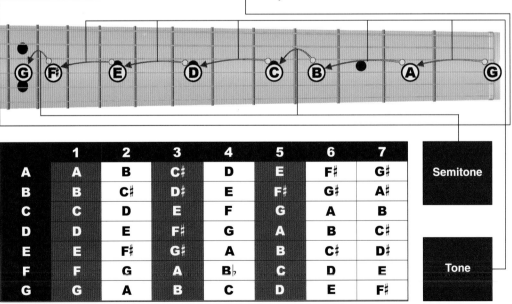

	1	2	3	4	5	6	7
A	A	B	C♯	D	E	F♯	G♯
B	B	C♯	D♯	E	F♯	G♯	A♯
C	C	D	E	F	G	A	B
D	D	E	F♯	G	A	B	C♯
E	E	F♯	G♯	A	B	C♯	D♯
F	F	G	A	B♭	C	D	E
G	G	A	B	C	D	E	F♯

Semitone

Tone

Keys

Keys take this process one step further by introducing a pattern of chords that matches the pattern of notes in the scale. It means that you are not limited to playing only the one chord consisting of the 1st, 3rd, and 5th notes of the scale you are in. For each note in the scale there is a chord that can also be played. These will be a major, minor, or diminished chord.

The pattern of chords for a major scale is:

Major, Minor, Minor, Major, Major, Minor, Diminished.

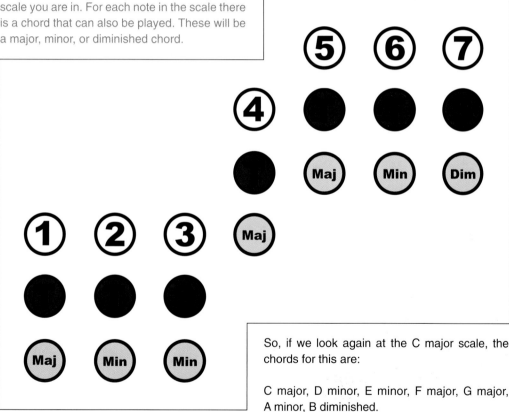

A diminished chord is similar to a minor chord but it has its 5th note flattened one semitone. This means that the 5th note is moved back one fret.

The difference between a major chord and a diminished one is that both the 3rd and 5th notes are flattened.

Diminished chords are not widely used in pop and rock music.

Major Chords	①③⑤
Minor Chords	①③♭⑤
Diminished Chords	①③♭⑤♭

So, if we look again at the C major scale, the chords for this are:

C major, D minor, E minor, F major, G major, A minor, B diminished.

Three-chord tricks

The 1st chord for a major scale is known as the Tonic chord.
The 5th chord is known as the Dominant chord.
The 4th chord is known as the Subdominant.

Most songs do not contain all of the chords in a particular key, often just using a few. As mentioned in Chapter Two, a lot of pop and rock songs rely on just three chords, referred to as three-chord tricks. The three chords used are not just any three chords in the key but again fall in a certain pattern.

If we go back and look at the chords we were using in the key of G major we can work out which chords should be used in a three-chord trick. We were using the G major, the C major and the D major. Using this pattern described above we can see that these are the 1st, 4th and 5th chords in the key of G major.

Top Far Right: G major chord
Bottom Far Right: C major chord
Right: D major chord

① ② ③ ④ ⑤ ⑥ ⑦
● ● ● ● ● ● ●
Ⓖ Ⓐ Ⓑ Ⓒ Ⓓ Ⓔ Ⓕ#
Maj Min Min Maj Maj Min Dim

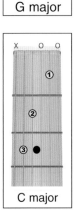

G major

C major

D major

C major scale

Let's now apply the same rules with the key of C that we learned at the beginning of this chapter.

The notes of this scale are C D E F G A B. So in the key of C major, the chords are:

C major, D minor, E minor, F major, G major, A minor and B diminished.

The 1st, 4th and 5th chords in this sequence are C major, F major and G major.

You have already learned how to play these chords. The C major and G major chords both appear in the key of G major, and the F major chord follows the same shape that was used for the first bar chord at the start of Chapter Three. To play the F major chord, place the bar chord at the 1st fret.

Left: F major chord ignoring the bottom E string

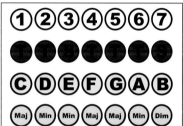

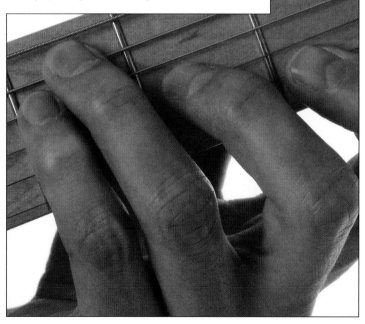

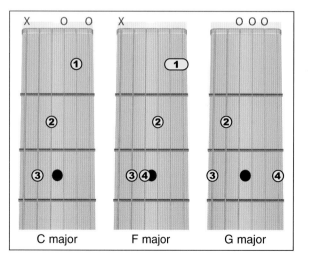

C major   F major   G major

Practice changing between the three chords, starting with the C major chord as this is the key we are in. Slowly start picking each string to make sure the notes play cleanly and then begin strumming while going through the chord changes. Try to keep the timing and pace even

and don't worry too much about fumbling the finger positions at first.

If you're having difficulties, it may be easier to ignore the bottom E string with the F major chord to allow for quicker changes between the three chords.

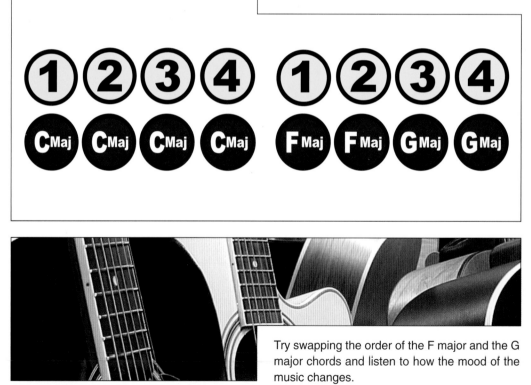

Try swapping the order of the F major and the G major chords and listen to how the mood of the music changes.

Moving to minor scales and keys

We've already heard how minor chords tend to sound sadder or more dramatic than major chords and this is also true for major and minor keys. Songs in a major key tend to sound bright and happy, while songs in a minor key tend to sound dark or melancholy. This is only a generalization though, as it is possible to write sad songs in a major key and happy songs in a minor key.

Reggae music, for example, is often written in a minor key, though the resulting song can be uplifting.

Minor scales also have a pattern to them but, unlike the major scale, there is more than one minor scale that can be used, to confuse matters slightly. For now we will use just the natural minor scale also known as the Aeolian scale.

It's all Greek to me

The Ancient Greeks noticed that different patterns of whole and half-step notes stimulated different emotions from audiences. They grouped these notes together as modes or scales and gave them names that were later adopted for use with modern western music. The Ionian and Aeolian scales are the most common.

The pattern of a natural minor scale is:

Tone, Semitone, Tone, Tone, Semitone, Tone, Tone

If we look at the scale for A minor this would be:
Starting with the root note of A.
One tone up is B.
A semitone up is C.
One tone up is D.
Another tone up is E.
A semitone up is F.
One tone up is G.
And the final tone returns us to A.

The A minor scale is A B C D E F G.

This is different from the A major scale which is A B C# D E F# G#.

The A minor scale resembles the C major scale as they share the same notes.

If you look closely at the pattern of the natural minor scale you can see that it is the same as that of the major scale, except that it starts at a different place, at the 6th note of the major scale.

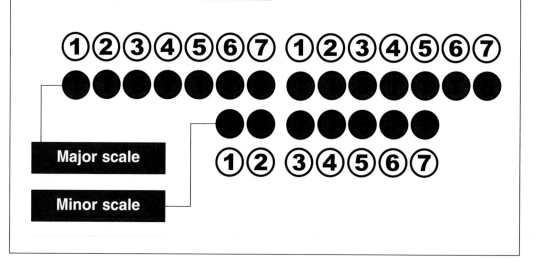

If you look along the notes of the C major scale you will see that the 6th note is an A.

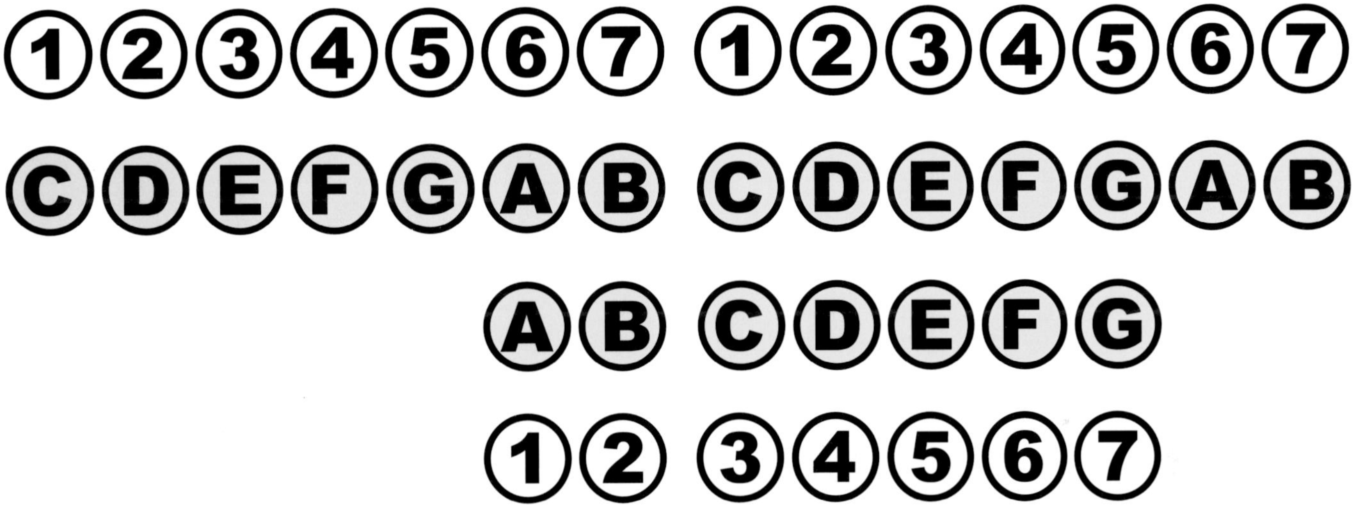

① ② ③ ④ ⑤ ⑥ ⑦   ① ② ③ ④ ⑤ ⑥ ⑦

C D E F G A B   C D E F G A B

A B C D E F G

① ② ③ ④ ⑤ ⑥ ⑦

Because they share the same notes, these two scales are related. The A minor scale is known as the relative minor scale of C major. Every major scale has a relative minor scale at its sixth position with which it shares its notes.

The minor chord is made up of the 1st, 3rd, and 5th notes of the minor scale, in this case the A, C, and E notes.

You could also say that the minor chord is made up of the 1st, flattened 3rd, and 5th notes of its major scale. In the case of creating an A minor, the major scale is A B C# D E F# G#, so the minor chord is A C E.

Remember that to flatten a note you move it one fret back down the neck.

A minor chord

Right: A minor chord

To play the A minor chord, place your index finger on the 1st fret of the B string to make a C note. Then place your second finger on the 2nd fret of the D string; this makes an E note. Finally, place your third finger on the 2nd fret of the G string to make an A note.

The bottom E string is usually left out of this chord. This is because there are already two E notes in the chord so it tends to dominate the sound. However, you can leave it in if you wish.

Don't forget to check that all the strings are playing cleanly before strumming the chord.

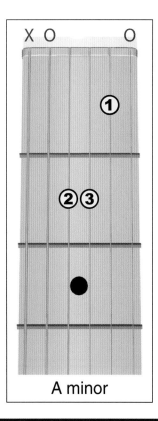

A minor

Before we explore more chords in the key of A minor, have a quick look again at the key of C major. You will notice that the 6th chord of

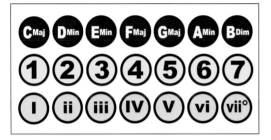

C major is in fact A minor. You can add this chord to the three you already have and extend the three-chord trick to four.

Try changing between the C major and A minor chords. This creates a pleasant sound and is also a very easy change as the third finger is the only one to move.

Now try extending this to include all four chords. A tune could repeat the C major to A minor change a few times and then use the G major and F major to resolve the sequence.

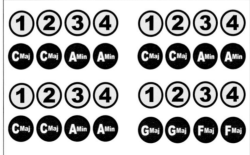

Roman numerals

*It is common to see the chords in a key written with Roman numerals.
The major chords are numbered using capital letters and the minor chords use lower case
letters. Diminished chords use lower case letters and have a degree symbol as well.*

Far Left: C major chord
Left: A minor chord

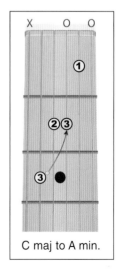

C maj to A min.

For a slightly different feel, try swapping the order of the last two chords. You could also try using a combination of up-strokes and down-strokes with your right hand to create more interesting rhythms.

This kind of chord sequence is typical of a verse section in a pop or rock song. A more dramatic use of the minor 6th chord would be to use it for a change from one chord sequence to another, such as the change from verse to chorus in a song. Try the sequence below to hear the kind of effect this has.

This more dramatic change is called a key change. We are changing from C major to its relative minor key, A minor. Even though we seem to be using the chords from the C major scale, the change from using the C major chord as the root to using the A minor chord as a root causes the effect of a key change.

Key changes between major keys and their relative minor keys are very popular in songwriting because, as well as sounding like a natural progression, the similarity between them makes it easy to remember the chords and easy to implement the changes. You often find verses played in one key and choruses in the related other key.

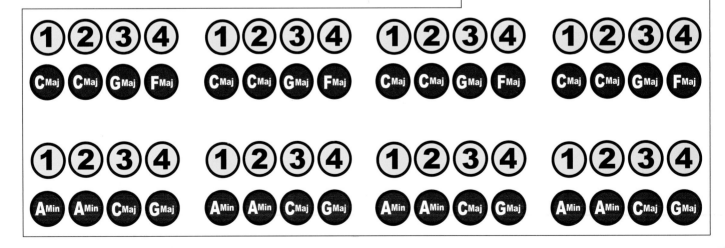

A minor scale

Now let's take a look at the rest of the chords in the key of A minor.

As you might expect, the pattern of chords for a natural minor key is similar to the major key relative to it as it is based upon the 6th note.

The pattern of chords for a minor key is: Minor, Diminished, Major, Minor, Minor, Major, Major.

This matches the pattern of chords in a major key, taken from its 6th position.

So the chords for the key of A minor are: A minor, B diminished, C major, D minor, E minor, F major and G major.

For the last chord sequence we used the 1st, 4th, and 5th chords from the C major key and then the 1st, 3rd, and 7th chords from A minor. Tunes that start in a minor key are often based on the 1st, 4th and 5th chords too, just as in the major keys.

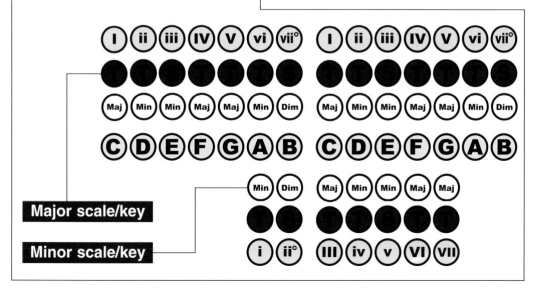

D minor chord

Let's now learn the 4th and 5th chords of the A minor key, the D minor, and E minor chords.

The scale of D minor is D, E, F, G, A, B flat, and C. So the D minor chord is made up of D, F, and A, the 1st, 3rd, and 5th notes of the scale.

To play a D minor chord, place your index finger on the 1st fret of the top E string, to make an F. The second finger goes on the 2nd fret of the G string to make an A, and the third finger is placed on the 3rd fret of the B string making a D.

It is usual to ignore the bottom two strings but you may want to include the A string for a heavier-sounding chord.

Right: D minor chord

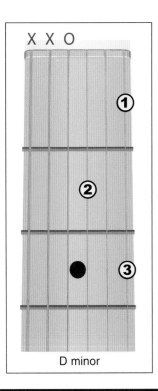

X X O

① ② ③

D minor

E minor chord

The scale of E minor is E, F#, G, A, B, C, D, giving the E minor chord the notes E, G, and B.

The E minor chord is one of the easiest to play. Place your index finger on the 2nd fret of the A string to make a B note. Then place your second finger on the 2nd fret of the D string to make an E. Play all the other strings open.

Try changing between the three chords, using similar patterns to the ones we used previously. Keep the timing even and the notes clean. Here is another pattern to try.

Left: E minor chord

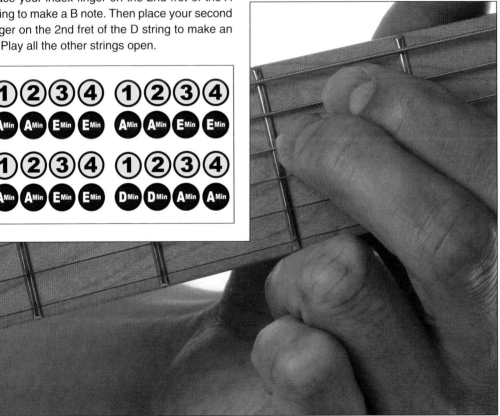

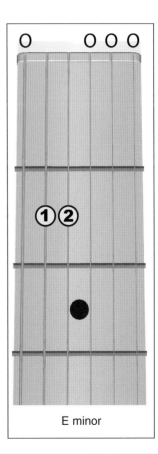

E minor

Now let's try to find the relative minor key to G major. If you look again at the scale for G major you can see that the 6th note is an E.

So the relative minor chord for G major is E minor, which is the one we have just been playing. Try adding E minor to the other chords we have been playing for G major.

You should practice playing through these chords in various combinations to see how well they fit together. Try playing the same pattern we used for C major but substituting the chords. Another exercise is at the bottom of the page.

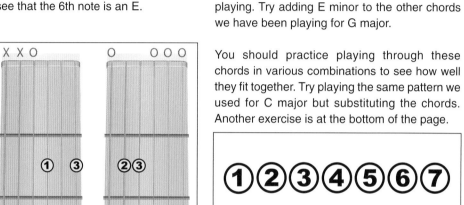

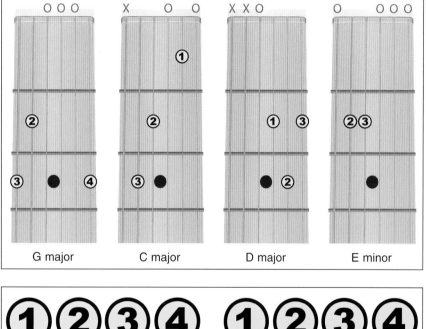

| G major | C major | D major | E minor |

Scale of G major

E minor key

Using what we already know about the relationship between the major scale and its relative minor, we can work out the scale for E minor.

Starting with the 6th note of the G major scale we get the notes E, F#, G, A, B, C, D. The chords in the key of E minor are E minor, F# diminished, G major, A minor, B minor, C major, and D major.

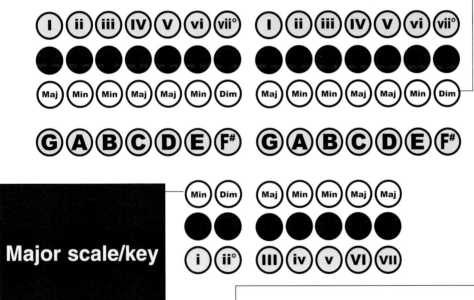

Our three-chord trick in this key uses E minor, A minor, and B minor, which introduces us to the new chord of B minor.

B minor chord

This chord is the same as the minor bar chord we created to be played on the A string. It is played two frets up the A string on the B note. The notes for B minor are B, D, and F sharp.

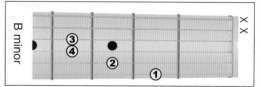

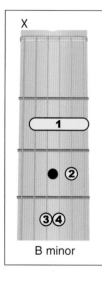

B minor

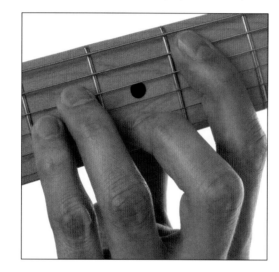

It may be easier to swap between the different chords if you ignore the two bottom strings of the B minor chord, as you won't have to bar across all the frets with the first finger. Place your index finger on the 2nd fret of the top E string, making an F#. Place your second finger on the 3rd fret of the B string to make a D. Place your third finger on the 4th fret of the D string to make an F# and your fourth finger also on the 4th fret but on the G string, making a B.

Right: B minor bar chord

Far Right: B minor bar chord ignoring the A and bottom E strings

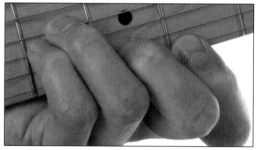

Try changing between these three chords by playing the sequence below. Increase the speed as you get used to the changes. You may find it takes a little time to get to the B minor from the other chords at first because it is a little further up the neck.

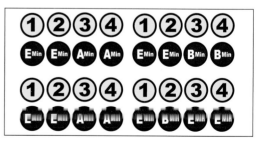

You now have four keys in your repertoire, two major and two minor ones. More importantly, you also know the formula for working out many more. We have explored changing keys between major keys and their relative minor keys to add some variation to our tunes.

If you want to start a tune in a minor key you can change key to its relative major, which appears at the third position of the scale. You can also count down the scale to the sixth position rather than up it to the third position to find the major scale.

Of course, you are not limited to using just the 1st, 4th, and 5th chords of a key to make a tune, but these are a good starting place to explore chord relationships and songwriting.

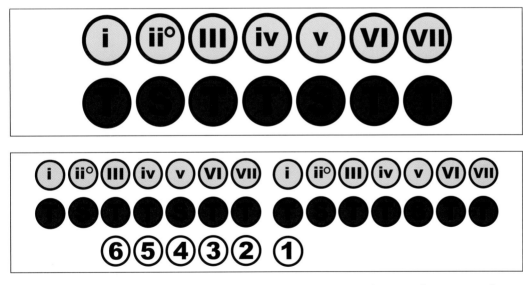

A good exercise is to analyze some of your favorite tunes by finding out the chord sequences used and working out which keys they are in and the pattern of chords used.

Tonal centers

Key changes within a song are not restricted to those between relative major and minor keys, but this is a good place to start because they use the same chords and notes. Key changes usually happen around a common chord found in both keys. This common chord is known as the tonal center.

For instance, you can change key from C major to G major or even E minor, by using one of the chords C major, G major, A minor, or E minor as the tonal center. As long as one of these chords features in both chord sequences a key change is valid.

Try the following chord sequence, which starts in G major and then changes to C major. The tonal center in this case is the chord C major as it appears in both sequences.

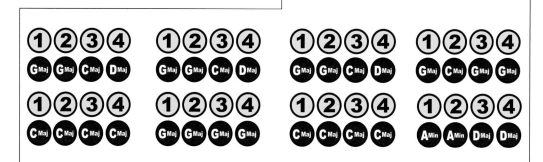

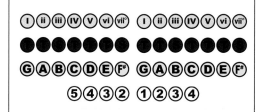

The key change described above moves to the IV position along the scale of G major. Key changes to positions IV and V are also very common.

A 4th up the scale is also known as a 5th down the scale.

The Circle of Fifths

There is a useful musical tool called the Circle of Fifths that helps you to see the relationships that exist between notes, chords and keys.

Across many cultures, the musical intervals of fourths and fifths have been considered pleasing to the ear and feature heavily in musical composition. The Ancient Greeks made many studies about the relationship of sound and music and many of their findings are still in use today. They discovered that the human ear is more sensitive to pitch ratios rather than changes in tone.

This is why octaves, fourths and fifths are most popular as the ratios are 2:1, 4:3 and 3:2. Tones built around these ratios are said to be consonant. The Circle of Fifths is a chart of twelve notes laid out in the form of a clock face. As you move round the chart in a clockwise direction you move through the major scales at intervals of fifths.

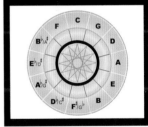

The Circle of Fifths contains all of the twelve possible notes in western music. If you look at the circle you can see that each semitone up is seven spaces clockwise from the previous tone and that each semitone down is five spaces counter-clockwise.

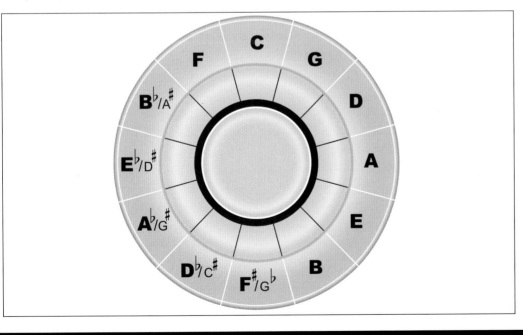

Fourths and fifths

The main use for this chart is to quickly find the most popular chords in each key. We have already established that fourths and fifths are the most popular intervals in each key. Looking again at the two major keys covered you can see that the fourth and fifth for C major are F and G, while the fourth and fifth for G major are C and D.

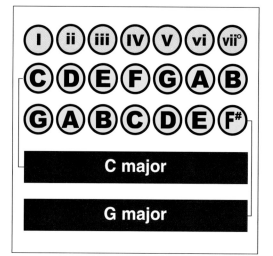

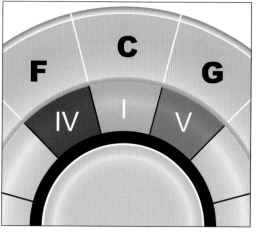

If you look at the position of C on the chart you will notice that F is one step anti-clockwise and G is one step clockwise, the fourth and fifth notes are either side of the root. Check again with the G and you will see the same pattern, the C is to the left and the D is to the right. This pattern holds true throughout the circle.

To quickly look up the most popular chords in any key, you pick your root note and the fourth and fifth either side of it. If you wanted to play a song in G# major, the most common chords to play with it would be C# major and D# major.

If you move clockwise around the circle you move in fifths and if you move anti-clockwise around the circle you move in fourths. Remember that a fourth is also known as being a fifth down the scale.

For major keys, the fourths and fifths are always major chords and for minor keys they are always minors. A fourth is five frets up the fretboard from the root note and a fifth is seven frets up.

Seven tones on the chart have enharmonic equivalents, which means that they have two names for the same note. When moving clockwise round the chart you use the sharp name for the note and when moving anti-clockwise you use the flattened name. The exception is B, which is not a sharp note but has a C flat equivalent.

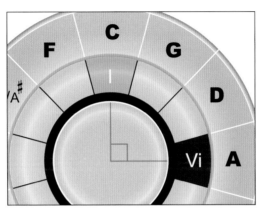

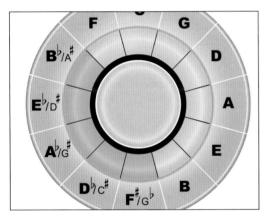

The other popular chord that we were looking at in the major scale was the minor chord at the 6th position, known as the relative minor. This chord is also easily located in the chart. The relative minor can be found 90° round the chart clockwise or you can count three places clockwise. So, the A minor chord which is the relative minor chord in the key of C major is three places clockwise from C.

Key changes are easy to spot on the chart as the most popular changes are to the fourth, fifth, and sixth positions. So if a tune starts in C major, the most popular key changes would be to F major, G major, or A minor. This pattern works all the way around the circle.

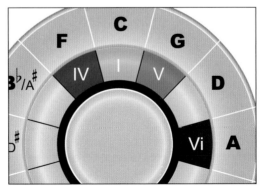

It is usual in written music to have the major chords represented by the chord letter and to have minor chords shown with a lower case "m" next to them.

As stated earlier, key changes can also take place where there is a tonal center, meaning that a particular chord appears in both the original key and the new key. This is easy to spot with the circle. If we stay with the C major key, its fifth is the G major and this chord is also shared with the D major key as it is the fourth of this key. So the key change between C and D is valid and would usually occur using the pivotal G major chord. The most common keys used in popular music are C, G, D, A, and E, the first five notes clockwise around the circle.

We should look at creating chords for the new keys in this list. If we refer to the Circle of Fifths we can see what the most popular chords are for these keys.

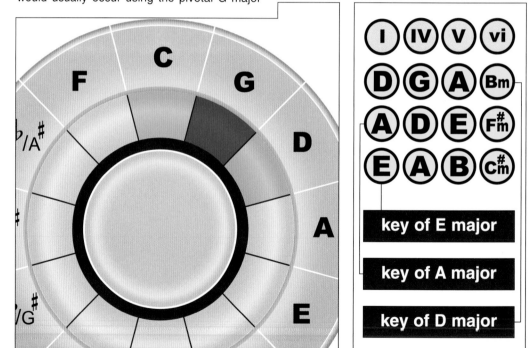

key of E major

key of A major

key of D major

Relative minor keys

We should also look at the relative minor keys for the major keys so that we can change key to them, too.

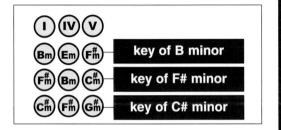

If we look through the list, we can isolate the chords that are new. These are the A major, B major, E major, C# minor, F# minor and G# minor. This gives us six new chords to learn, three major chords and three minor chords.

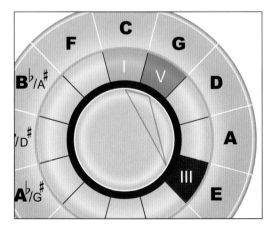

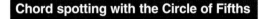

Chord spotting with the Circle of Fifths

You can use the Circle of Fifths to work out the notes that make up major and minor chords. To show the notes for a major chord you can draw a triangle from the root note to the third note of the scale, which is four steps clockwise and then to the fifth note of the scale, which is three steps back from this note. In the case of C major this gives you C, E and G.

For minor chords, the triangle is reversed so that you go three steps anti-clockwise to find the third note and then four steps clockwise from this point to find the fifth. In this case, it gives us the notes C, D# and G.

You can rotate these triangles around the circle to work out the notes for any of the chords.

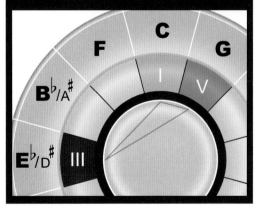

A major chord

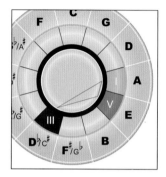

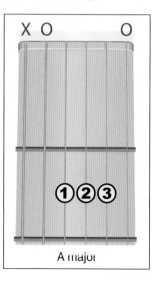

Right: A major chord
Far Right: A major bar chord
ignoring both E strings

Let us now look at creating the new major chords. If we refer to the circle to work out the notes for A major, we start with our root note of A then move clockwise four steps to C# and then back three steps to E. The notes for the A major chord are A, C#, and E.

To create this chord, place your index finger on the 2nd fret of the D string to make an E note. The second finger goes on the 2nd fret of the G string to make an A and the third finger also goes on the 2nd fret but on the B string to make a C#.

It may be a bit of a squeeze fitting all your fingers into one fret space, so you may have to offset your fingers slightly. Try placing your index finger further back in the space between the 1st and 2nd fret, then place the second finger just in front of the first and the third finger just in front of the second.

Alternatively, you could just bar across the 2nd fret with your index finger and ignore the top E string. The bottom E string is usually ignored.

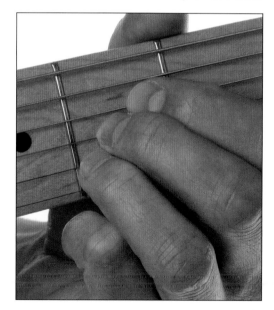

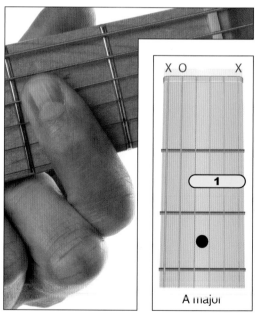

A major

A major

E major chord

Sliding our chord triangle round the circle we can work out that the notes for the E major chord are E, G# and B.

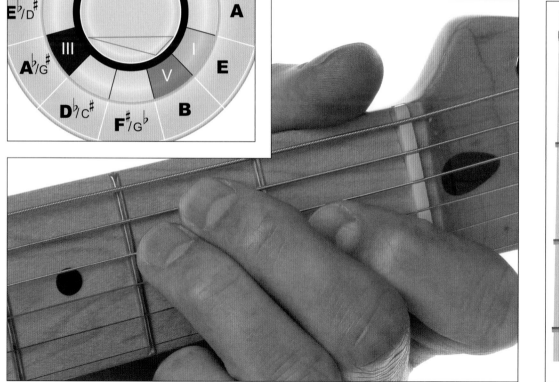

To create the E major chord, place your index finger on the 1st fret of the G string to turn it into a G#. Then place your second finger on the 2nd fret of the A string to make a B and then your third finger on the 2nd fret of the D string to make an E. This is very similar to the E minor chord.

Left: E major chord

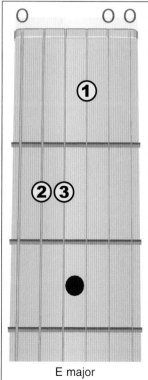

E major

B major chord

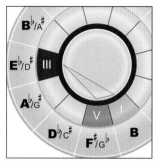

Right: B major bar chord
Far Right: B major double bar chord

Using our chord triangle again, we see that the notes for B major are B, D#, and F#.

The B major chord is the same as the major bar chord for the A string and is played on the 2nd fret.

Use the first finger to bar across the top five strings of the 2nd fret. This will make a B on the A string and an F# on the top E string. Then place the second, third, and fourth fingers on the 4th frets of the D, G, and B strings, making the notes F#, B, and D# respectively.

This chord is the same shape as the A major chord but moved two frets up the neck.

You may be able to bar the 4th fret with your third finger across the D, G, and B strings.

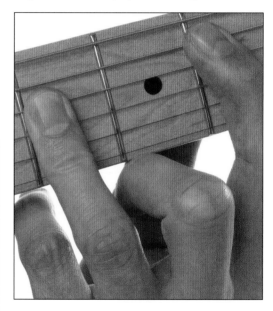

B major

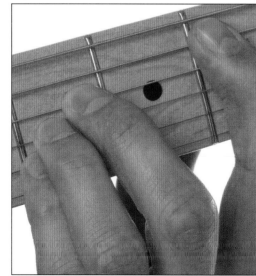

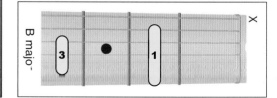

B majo-

Alternatively, you can ignore the A string along with the bottom E and use your index finger on just the top E string.

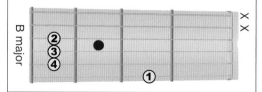

Before moving on to learn the minor chords, take a break and play around with the major chords we have just created.

The following sequence changes key between D major and E major and uses the A major chord as the common chord between them.

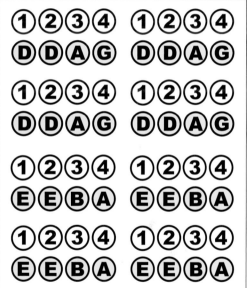

It may take a while to be able to change between A major and B major quickly enough to keep the timing, so experiment by using partial chords and bars to help you.

Left: B major chord ignoring the A string

C# minor chord

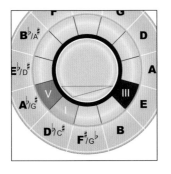

Right: C# minor chord

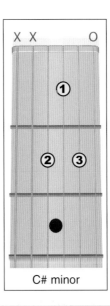

C# minor

Let's now explore the minor chords that complete the relative minor keys.

We can use the second chord triangle on the Circle of Fifths to find the notes required to make the minor chords. It's three steps anti-clockwise, followed by four steps clockwise.

By rotating the triangle to the C# position on the circle, you can see that the C# minor chord is made up of C#, E, and G# notes.

To create this chord, place your index finger on the 1st fret of the G string to make a G#. Then place your second finger on the 2nd fret of the D string to make an E. Your third finger goes on the 2nd fret of the B string to make C#. You should ignore the bottom two strings.

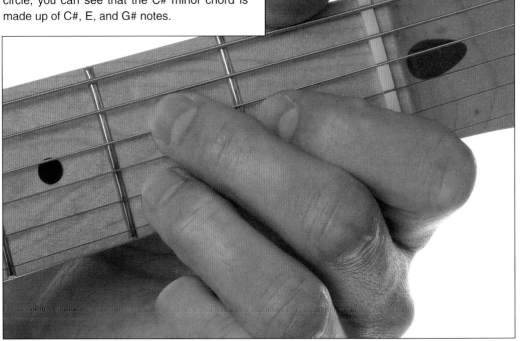

F# minor chord

Rotating the minor chord triangle round to the F# note, you can see that the notes for the minor chord are F#, A, and C#.

You can ignore the bottom E string to make it slightly easier to play, as we already have two F#s in the chord.

Top: F# minor bar chord
Bottom: F# minor ignoring the bottom E string

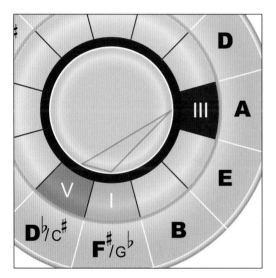

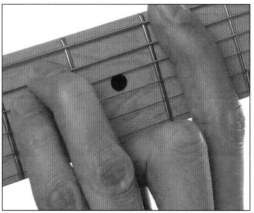

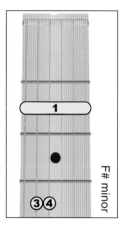

To form the F# minor chord, we use the minor chord bar shape for the E string.

Start by barring your index finger across all the strings at the 2nd fret, making an F# on both the E strings as well as an A on the G string and a C# on the B string. Then place your third finger on the 4th fret of the A string making another C#. The fourth finger goes just below on the 4th fret of the D string to make an F#.

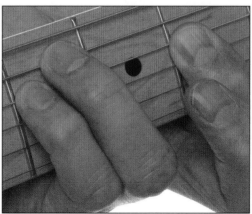

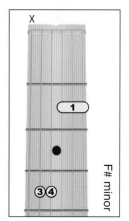

G# minor chord

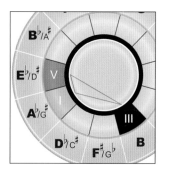

If we rotate the minor chord triangle round two more steps clockwise to the G# position we get the notes for the G# minor chord. They are G#, B, and D#.

To play this chord, slide the last chord shape up the neck by two frets to the 4th fret. The first finger creates G# notes on the E strings and B and D# on the G and B strings. The third finger makes a D# and the fourth a G#. Again, you can leave out the top E string, if you prefer.

Here is an exercise that uses some of the new chords. It starts in the key of C# minor and then changes to its relative major key of E.

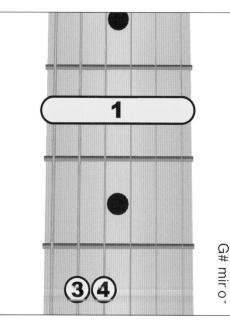

G# minor

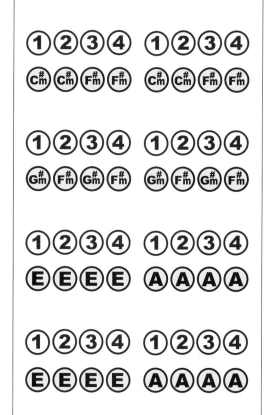

Transposing

To try out some of the keys that we have covered, we can transpose rhythms to new keys using the Circle of Fifths.

If we analyze the components of the last rhythm, we will see that the first two parts alternate between the root and its fourth. The second two parts alternate between the fifth and fourth chords. It then changes key to its relative major key and alternates between the major key's root and its fourth.

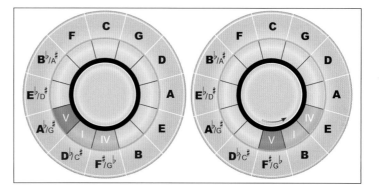

The tune uses different chords but keeps the same relationships between them.

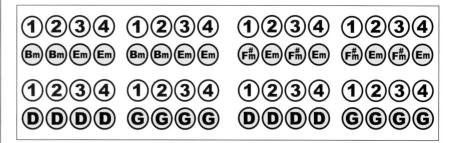

We can easily transpose this piece of music to another key by looking at the pattern it makes on the Circle of Fifths and then rotating the pattern to a new point. So if you wanted to play the same rhythm, but in the key of B minor, rotate the pattern two steps counter-clockwise.

Try transposing some of the other rhythms that we have been practicing into new keys.

Transposition is a useful skill as it is sometimes necessary to transpose a song to a new key if an instrument or singer can't reach certain notes within the key that it is currently in.

Extended chords

Once you feel comfortable playing major and minor chords you may want to experiment with more complex chords. So far, we have only been using three-note chords, referred to as triads, but you can have chords with four or more notes in them. These are usually known as "extended chords."

A lot of guitarists avoid extended chords, believing them to be too difficult and so ignore any extra symbols in chord diagrams and music sheets. However, once you understand how extended chords are created you will realize that they are not that much more difficult than triads.

Chords are based on harmonies, notes that work well together. The triads that we have looked at so far are made up of alternative notes in the 1st, 3rd, and 5th of a scale. This can be extended through the scale to include 7ths, 9ths, 11ths, and even 13ths. This is done by repeating the seven-note scale, so a 9th is equivalent to a 2nd, an 11th to a 4th, and a 13th to a 6th.

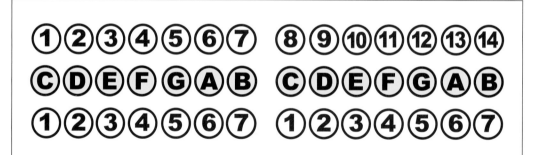

C major 7th chord

The extended chord of C major to include the seventh note of the scale is referred to as a C major 7th, or Cmaj7 chord. It is made up of C, E, G, and B notes. As more notes get added to a chord, the number of ways of forming it increases. It is best to try a few variations to work out which one fits into the tune in terms of sound and how easy it is to change between the different chords involved.

Here is one version of the Cmaj7 chord that is quite easy to play. When choosing which notes to include in the chord, you must include at least one B to make it a 7th.

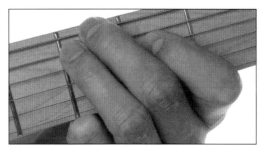

There is another version of the Cmaj7 chord that can be used as a bar chord with the root note based upon the note held by the first finger on the A string.

Major 7th chords have a light and happy sound to them and were commonly used in popular music during the Sixties.

Top: C major 7 chord
Bottom: C major 7 bar chord

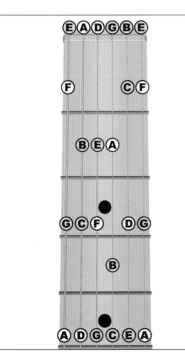

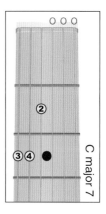

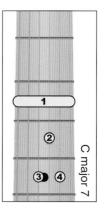

Dominant chords

Although major 7ths can be used in songwriting, dominant chords are used much more often.

A dominant 7th chord is almost the same as a major 7th but the 7th note is flattened. This means that the 7th note is placed one fret back. A C7 chord consists of the notes C, E, G, and A#. (Remember that A sharp is the same as B flat.)

This gives the chord a note that is not in the scale of C major. Dominant 7ths are sometimes referred to as "flattened 7ths."

Dominant chords are written using a number after the note name, such as C7 or C9, whereas major chords always include the word major in them, such as in Cmaj7.

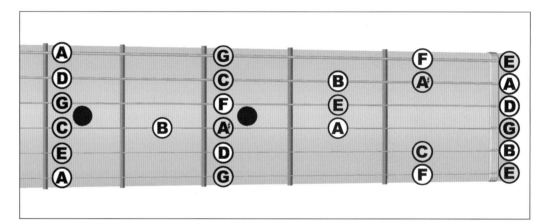

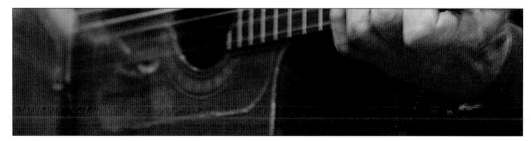

C7 chord

Try this version of the C7 chord and listen to the sound it makes. The flattened 7th gives the chord an unresolved feel, a sound that seems to need to be followed by another chord. Try changing between C7 and F major to hear the effect.

It is usual for the chord at position V in the scale to be a turned into a dominant 7th chord. Three-chord tricks often use the dominant 7th chord because it resolves to the root chord.

Left: C7 chord

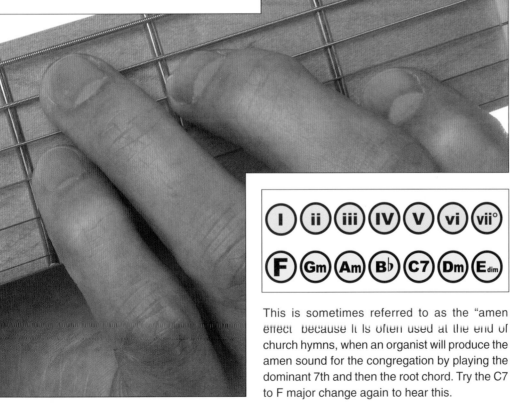

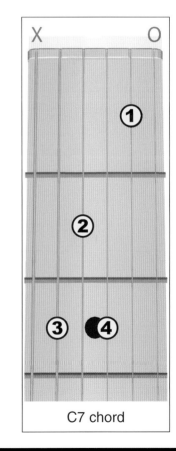

C7 chord

I	ii	iii	IV	V	vi	vii°
F	Gm	Am	Bb	C7	Dm	Edim

This is sometimes referred to as the "amen effect" because it is often used at the end of church hymns, when an organist will produce the amen sound for the congregation by playing the dominant 7th and then the root chord. Try the C7 to F major change again to hear this.

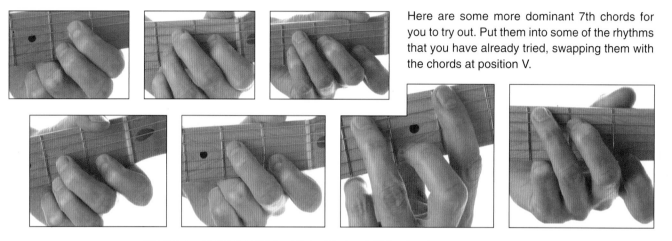

Here are some more dominant 7th chords for you to try out. Put them into some of the rhythms that you have already tried, swapping them with the chords at position V.

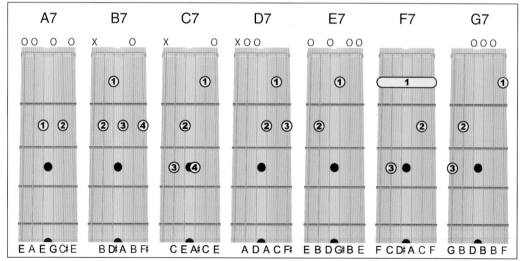

A7	B7	C7	D7	E7	F7	G7
O O O O	X O	X O	X O O	O O OO		O O O

Top Row: A7, B7, C7 chords
Bottom Row: D7, E7, F7, G7 chords

E A E G C♯ E   B D♯ A B F♯   C E A♯ C E   A D A C F♯   E B D G♯ B E   F C D♯ A C F   G B D B B F

You can create dominant minor 7th chords in exactly the same way, by working out the 7th note in the minor scale and flattening it. These chords will also resolve to their root chord.

Minor chords can have major 7ths, in which cases they are referred to as minor major 7ths, but their use is rare.

Clockwise From Top: G minor 7 chord on 3rd fret, F minor 7 chord, E minor 7 chord, D minor 7 chord, C minor 7 chord

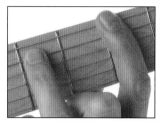

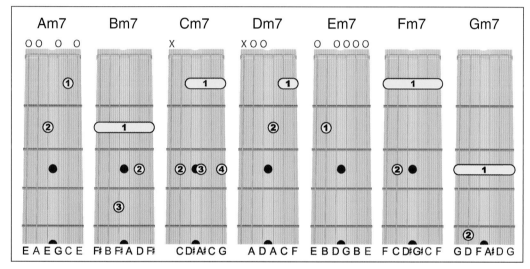

Am7	Bm7	Cm7	Dm7	Em7	Fm7	Gm7
O O O O		X	X O O	O O O O O		

E A E G C E | F♯ B F♯ A D F♯ | C D♯ A♯ C G | A D A C F | E B D G B E | F C D♯ G♯ C F | G D F A♯ D G

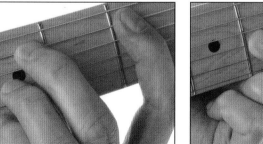

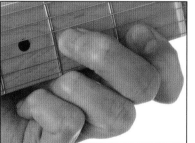

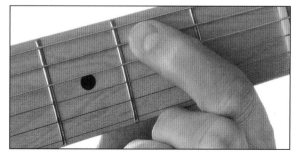

The reason these chords are called "dominant 7ths" is because the 5th note in a scale is called the "dominant note." All the notes in a scale have their own name.

You can add a flattened 7th note to any chord, but the sound it makes always seems to lead you to resolve it to a chord that is a IV away from it, making the flattened 7th chord a V of the resolving chord's scale.

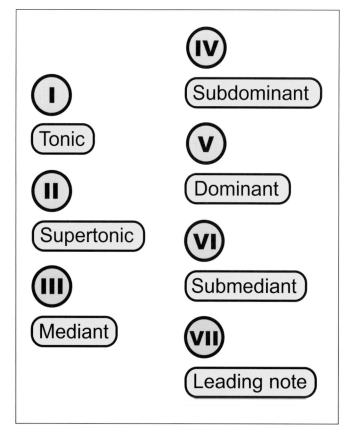

You can link together dominant 7th chords and go round the Circle of Fifths, but you will always need to resolve to a major or minor triad as in, D7-G7-C7-F, the resolving chord being F major. This technique is called "modulation" because it temporarily moves through other keys.

The blues

7th notes can be added to major or minor chords as you play, a technique often used in blues music. Try the following sequence, holding the major chords and adding or altering to the dominant 7th chord as you play.

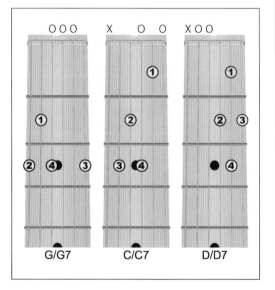

G/G7   C/C7   D/D7

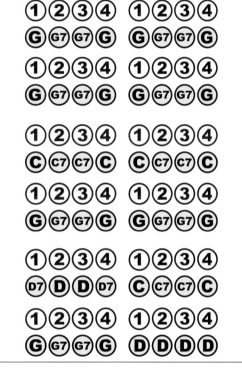

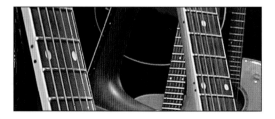

The above sequence uses twelve parts of four beats to cycle through the 1st, 4th, and 5th chords of the key. This sequence is called the "12-bar blues" and is the basis of most rock music. The flattened 7th is very useful for adding a blues or jazz music feel to a tune and it is often called a "blue note."

Playing 9ths

The 9th chords are dominant 7th chords with a 9th or 2nd note added to them.

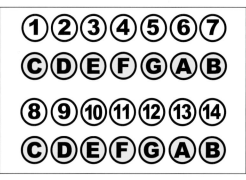

A C9 chord would use the notes C, E, G, A#, D. Because a 9th note is the same as a 2nd note, 9th chords are sometimes created by moving one or more of the root notes up the neck by two frets.

There is a barred version of the 9th chord that is commonly used. The root note is taken from the placement of the index finger on the bottom E string, so the C9 chord will appear on the 8th fret.

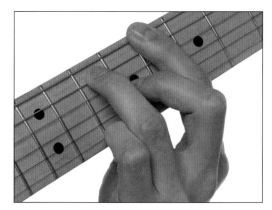

Right: C9 chord
Far Right: C9 bar chord on the 8th fret

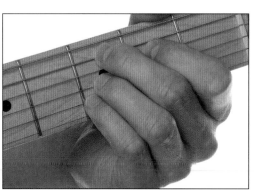

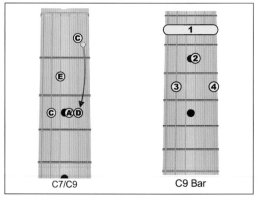

C7/C9

C9 Bar

11th and 13th chords

The 11th and 13th chords take this process further by adding more notes to the dominant 7th chord. A C11 chord would have the notes C, E, G, A#, D, and F. A C13 chord contains the notes C, E, G, A#, D, F, and A. Clearly there are practical problems with trying to form these chords with only four fingers and six strings available, particularly as the 13th contains seven notes.

It is common to leave the root note out of a chord when playing in a band, as it is usually being played by another instrument, typically the bass guitar. It is also common to leave out the 5th note of a chord. The 3rd note should not be taken out as it determines whether the chord is major or minor. The eleventh note in a 13th chord can also be ignored.

Looking at the bar chords that we created, we can see how the addition of notes will affect the chord shape.

Top: C7 bar chord on the 8th fret
Bottom Left: C9 bar chord
Bottom Middle: C11 bar chord
Bottom Right: C13 bar chord

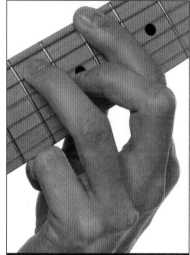

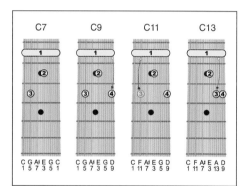

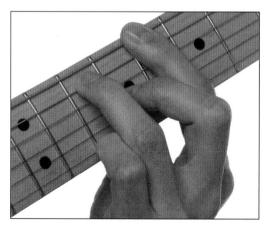

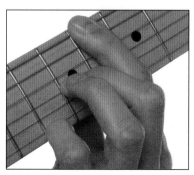

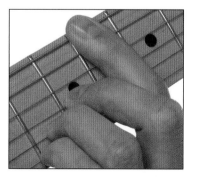

The more notes you add to chords, the more ways there are to play them. With triad chords, there are only a few ways of arranging the notes to form chords, but with 13ths there can be dozens of ways to form them. Have a look at the diagram of all the notes on the neck and try creating some for yourself from the scales we have already covered.

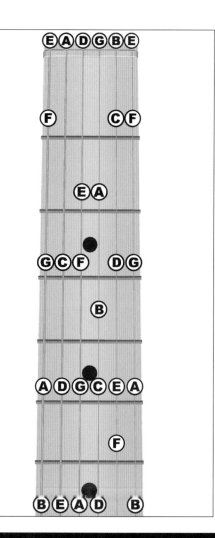

	1	2	3	4	5	6	7	8	9	10	11	12	13
A	A	B	C#	D	E	F#	G#	A	B	C#	D	E	F#
B	B	C#	D#	E	F#	G#	A#	B	C#	D#	E	F#	G#
C	C	D	E	F	G	A	B	C	D	E	F	G	A
D	D	E	F#	G	A	B	C#	D	E	F#	G	A	B
E	E	F#	G#	A	B	C#	D#	E	F#	G#	A	B	C#
F	F	G	A	B♭	C	D	E	F	G	A	B♭	C	D
G	G	A	B	C	D	E	F#	G	A	B	C	D	E

Extended chords can be substituted for any regular major or minor triad in a tune to add a different feel to the tune. Then it is up to you to experiment to find a sound that suits you.

Reading and Writing Music

If you intend to take your guitar-playing further than strumming a few chords, sooner or later you are going to need to know how to read music and this means studying some music theory.

This chapter gives you a brief look at how music is written and read. We will look at notes, staves, clefs, and other musical symbols, as well as alternative methods of reading and writing music, such as chord boxes and guitar tablature.

We will start off with a brief recap of what we already know about music:

1. There are seven whole notes that run from A through G.

2. There is a total of twelve possible notes including all sharps and flats.

3. A scale is a sequence of notes that follows a specific pattern.

4. The relative minor scale uses the same notes as those of its major scale.

5. Scales repeat themselves getting higher or lower in pitch each time they loop around, so that every repeated note is an octave higher or lower than the previous one.

6. A key allows you to play a set of chords based on the notes that appear in a scale.

We shall start by looking at the way music has traditionally been written before approaching the relatively new concepts of chord boxes and guitar tablature.

A sheet of music can be quite daunting if you've never been taught how to read it, but once you learn a few of the rules of written notation, it should soon become decipherable.

It is a lot easier to read music than it is to write it, as you can make sense of most music notation without really understanding all of the symbols or being able to read it fluently. However, writing music notation so that other people can understand it takes great care and attention to detail. Fortunately, there are a number of computer software packages that can aid you in writing music, though for most people it is enough to be able to make a few notes as a reminder of a tune or to communicate an idea to another musician.

It takes a lot of work to get to the stage where you can sight-read music, meaning you are able to pick up a sheet of music and play the tune straight away. You should expect to work your way through a piece of music very slowly at first, reading each note one at a time.

Staves

Music is written on sets of parallel lines called staves. There are five lines with four spaces between them, each line and space representing a different note.

Dots are placed along the lines and spaces to show which notes are to be played. The music is read, like a book, from left to right.

Different symbols will also be placed at the beginning of a stave to indicate which sets of notes the lines and spaces represent.

Clefs

The first symbol to appear on a line of music is always a clef. The two most common clefs are the treble clef and the bass clef. The pitch that the music will be played in and the notes that are represented by the lines and spaces will alter according to which clef is used.

The treble clef tells you that the music on the stave has been written for higher notes. This is the most common clef seen in guitar music.

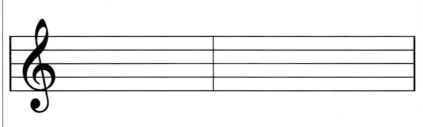

A bass clef tells you that the notes on its stave are all low notes.

The bass clef often appears below the treble clef in music notation on a separate stave for bass players to read. It is never interchanged with the treble clef on the same stave.

Two or more staves are often joined together with a line to show that they form one piece of music.

Both clefs are used for piano and keyboard music, with the bass clef representing what the left hand should be doing and the treble clef representing the right hand. Music written for keyboards has a bracket at the beginning of the music that joins the two staves together to show that they are linked to the same instrument. The bar lines throughout the piece of music are also joined.

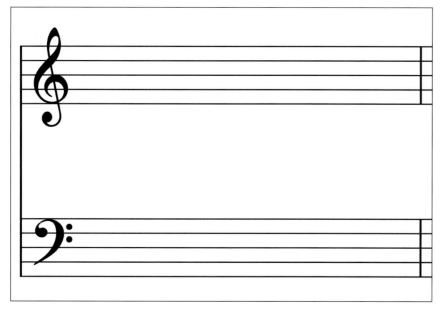

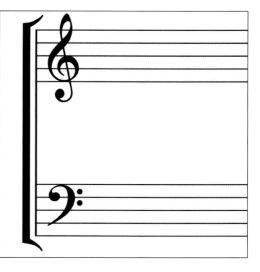

The clef is usually included at the beginning of every new line of music for easy reference.

There are other clefs that are used for instruments with different pitches but we don"t need to bother with them here. They can be found by looking at any basic music theory book, if you are interested.

The notes of the treble clef

The treble clef is also known as the G clef, not because it resembles the letter G but because the curl of the clef wraps around the line that represents the G note.

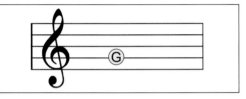

Each line and space represents a different whole note, with lower notes at the bottom of the stave and higher notes at the top. The notes always rise in alphabetical order.

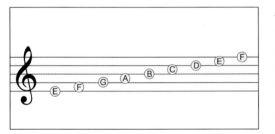

There are various ways to remember which notes appear on which lines. One is to remember that the treble clef wraps around the line representing G. You can make up an acronym to remember the notes on the lines of the stave, for example, "Every Good Boy Deserves Favors."

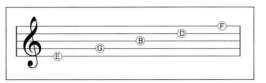

The notes that fall in between the lines spell FACE from bottom to top.

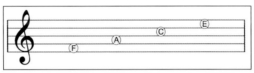

The notes of the bass clef

The bass clef is known as the F clef because it curls around the line that represents the F note on that stave. It also has two dots that are either side of the F line.

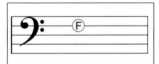

As with the treble clef, the notes on the bass clef rise from the bottom in alphabetical order.

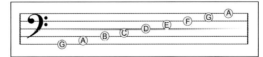

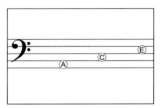

You will notice that the notes on the bass clef differ from those on the treble clef.

Leger lines

When a piece of music has notes that are higher or lower in pitch than the staves will allow, leger, or ledger, lines are used.

These give each clef a three-octave range. If notes need to go beyond this range then an "8" or "8va" is written above or below the stave with a dotted or continuous line showing the range of notes affected. The line ends with a right angle.

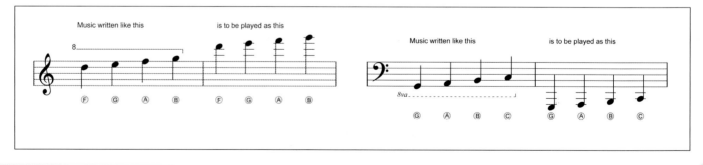

Middle C

The notes of the treble and bass clefs overlap at what is called "middle C." The position of middle C is one leger line below the treble clef and one leger line above the bass clef.

Music will never be written like this with notes crossing between the staves. Leger and the 8va symbols are always used to avoid confusion. This is also true with keyboard music where the staves seem to be joined.

Most guitar music is written using the treble stave, so we will concentrate on that one from this point on.

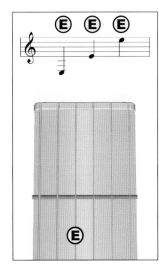

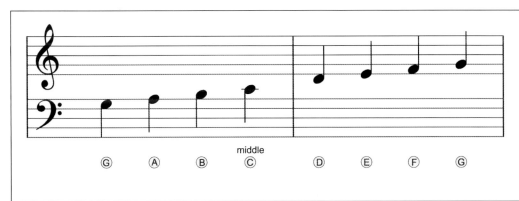

Finding notes on the guitar

We now know what notes are written along a stave, but we need to find out where they should be played on the guitar, otherwise we could be playing the correct notes but in the wrong octave, or register, as it is usually referred to. It is easy to remember that the line of G that the

treble clef wraps around is the same as the open G string on the guitar. Have a look at the note placements of all the open strings.

You should see now that the distance between the two E strings is two octaves.

Note values

You should now be able to work out the notes on a stave and find them on the neck of a guitar. We now need to look at how to figure out the rhythm of a piece of music, by finding out how long we should hold each note before going on to the next.

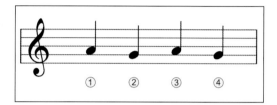

There are different types of dots, each of which has their own value and name. The basic black note with a stem attached is called a crotchet. It has a value of one and is sometimes referred to as a "quarter note."

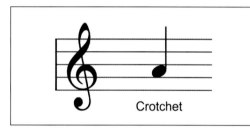

Crotchet

The value of each note relates to the way we count when playing music. In the earlier exercises that we practiced with chord sequences we were counting in fours. Each count has the same time value as a crotchet, making each section or bar of music equal in time to four crotchets. All the other notes have time values that are multiples or fractions of the basic crotchet value of one. If we look at some more notes this will become clearer.

A minim is the next note up in value from a crotchet and it has a length of two. It looks slightly different from the crotchet as it has a hollow dot. A minim is also known as a half-note.

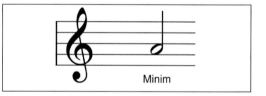

Minim

The minim lasts for two counts, as it has a value of two.

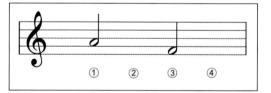

It is important to note that the sound of the note continues or sustains for the duration of the count of two and there is no rest between the notes.

Let's now look at a quaver note, which has a note value equal to half a crotchet and is also known as an eighth note. A quaver looks similar to a crotchet but has a small tail attached to the stem of the note. This tail is also called a flag.

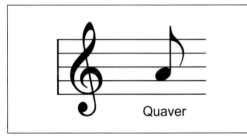

Quaver

The value of a quaver is a half so it lasts for half a count. You count half-notes or beats by inserting the word "and" in between the numbers, keeping the time between the numbers the same.

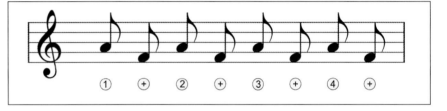

You will now be able to tell the rhythm of the music, by working out how long to hold a note for before playing the next one.

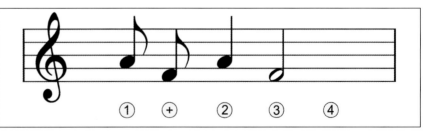

If you want to leave spaces or rests in between the notes, there are symbols to indicate these as well. Each note has its own equivalent symbol that can be inserted instead of the note for a rest of the same length. Here is a complete list of notes, their values, and rests.

Note	Name	Note Value	Rest	Count Value
Semibreve		1		4
Minim		1/2		2
Crotchet		1/4		1
Quaver		1/8		1/2
Semiquaver		1/16		1/4
Demisemiquaver		1/32		1/8
Hemidemisemiquaver		1/64		1/16

The stem of a note, if it has one, points upward if the note is on the lower half of the stave and downward if it is on the upper half of the stave. If a note lies on the middle line of the stave it can point in either direction, depending on which way the stems of the notes on either side of it are pointing.

The tails of the smaller value notes always appear on the right-hand side of the stem. Notes with a value of a quaver or less usually have their tails joined together so that they add up to the value of a crotchet or one beat. This makes recognizing the number of notes and their values easier.

Time signature

Another aid to describing rhythm is a time signature. This is a pair of numbers at the beginning of a stave that lets you know what kind of rhythm to count while playing the notes. It also allows the stave to be divided up into bars.

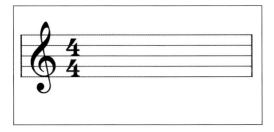

The upper number tells you how many beats or counts there are to a bar. If the upper number is a four you count from one to four for each bar. If the number is a three you count from one to three, and so on.

The lower number tells you what type of note to use with the count. The number is not the note value but refers to how many of the notes would make up a whole note or "semibreve", which is equal in length to four crotchets or two minims. So having a four as the bottom number means that each beat should be equal to a quarter-note or crotchet. A number two at the bottom would mean that half-notes or minims were required, and an eight would mean eighth notes or quavers.

4
4 means four beats to the bar with each beat equal to a crotchet

4
2 means four beats to the bar with each beat equal to a minim

4
8 means four beats to the bar with each beat equal to a quaver

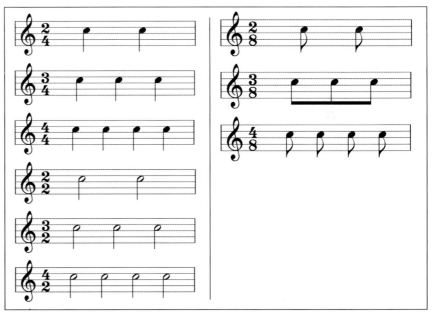

Four-four timing is the most popular time signature, particularly in pop and rock music. It is also called Common Time and sometimes there is a C on the stave instead of the numbers to indicate four-four time.

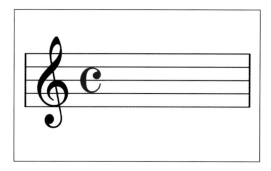

Each bar in a piece of music must contain notes and rests equivalent in value to the number set out on the top half of the time signature. When that value has been reached, a line is drawn to start a new bar. This enables you to read the music quickly and to keep your place in it.

Time signatures can change during a piece of music but the change will always occur at the beginning of a bar. A double line is drawn at the end of the preceding bar to signify a change.

Ties

If a note has to be held for longer than the length of a bar, then the note is split into smaller notes, which are then joined with a tie, represented by a curved line between the notes.

Tied notes should be played as a single note lasting for the duration of the combined value of the tied notes. You will sometimes see two tied notes on different lines of the stave. This means

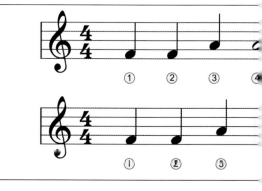

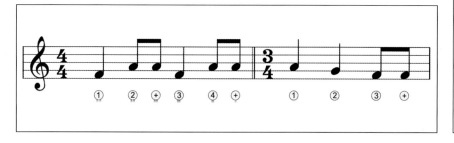

Accidentals

that two notes are played as one by sliding your finger from one fret to the next.

The stave only allows for natural notes—those that are not sharps or flats. Sharp or flat notes have their corresponding symbol placed just before them on their natural line. These symbols are called accidentals.

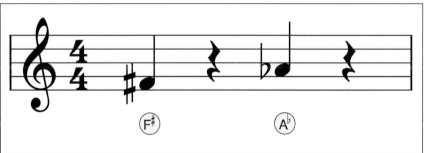

When an accidental has been used, its effect continues for the duration of the bar and affects any other notes on that line. The effect is canceled when either a natural symbol appears or the bar comes to an end.

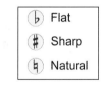

♭	Flat
♯	Sharp
♮	Natural

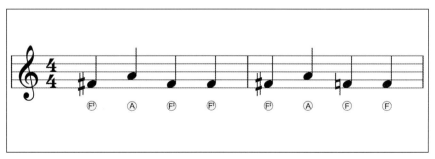

Dotted notes

Repeated sections

Sometimes you will see notes with a dot after them. This means that the value of the note and its duration is extended by half again. This gives you access to notes of odd durations. A minim with a dot is worth three rather than two. A crotchet with a dot is worth one and a half, and a quaver with a dot is worth three quarters. The value of the bar should still not be exceeded when using dotted notes.

You will often find that parts of music within a tune need to be repeated. Rather than writing out the section again, repeat symbols can be used to indicate which parts are to be repeated. Double lines with double dots are written at the beginning and end of the sections that need to be repeated. You will often find these at the end of a song where sections are repeated until the music fades out. Large repeat sections can sometimes be found where verses in a song are exactly the same and so the music can be played again, while the words may be changed.

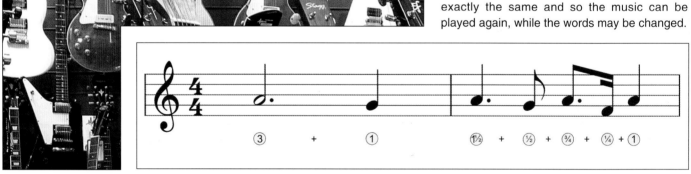

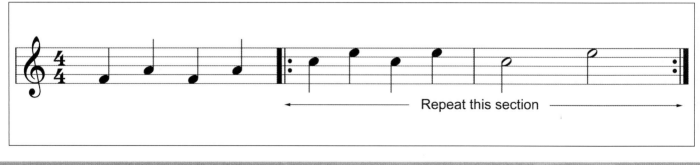

Repeat this section

Tempo

We now have a fairly good idea about how to interpret rhythm from written music notation, but we need something that tells us how fast the rhythm should be played.

The speed or tempo of music is usually displayed just above the first stave. There is a symbol of a note being equal to a number. The note symbol is the one indicated by the bottom number in the time signature. The number is the tempo and it tells you how many of the notes should be played every minute. If the tempo is 120, then 120 notes or beats are played per minute; this can be written as 120bpm.

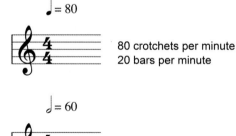

Chords

To display chords in written music you must stack the notes of the chord on top of each other and give them a single stem and tail if needed. You may sometimes see the name of the chord also written below the music—this could be below the bass clef.

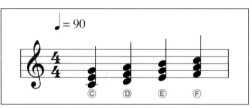

Chord boxes

It is quite common in popular music-books to have chord boxes along the tops of the staves to show you how the chords are played on the guitar, as the chords in the music may be written as they are supposed to be played on a keyboard.

The boxes have six vertical lines representing the strings from bottom E to top E and four or five horizontal lines representing the frets. Along the top of the box an o may be used to indicate an open string and an x for a blocked or ignored string. The name of the chord is usually displayed above the box.

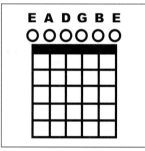

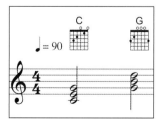

Key signatures

The final piece of the music notation puzzle is the most complex and it addresses the issue of how we work out the key in which the music is to be played. Let's refresh our memories about scales and keys.

We have already established that music is played in keys—where certain notes and chords are played harmoniously together, eliminating some of the guesswork of what to play.

A key is based upon the notes in a scale and the scale is a specific pattern of notes, starting with a root note. Both the key and scale take their basic name from the root note (for example, C major, F# minor) and the scale denotes the exact key (for example, C major, F# minor).

The major scale is based on a pattern of whole and half tones and each major scale has a relative minor scale that shares the same notes.

The pattern for a major scale is Tone Tone Semitone Tone Tone Tone Semitone. A semitone is one fret distance and a tone is two. Using this pattern, we can work out the scales using the neck of the guitar.

C major scale works out as C D E F G A B C
G major scale works out as G A B C D E F# G
D major scale works out as D E F# G A B C# D
A major scale works out as A B C# D E F# G# A

As you can see, a pattern is developing. Each scale listed has one more sharp note in it than the previous one. The order of the scales presented matches the notes moving clockwise around the Circle of Fifths.

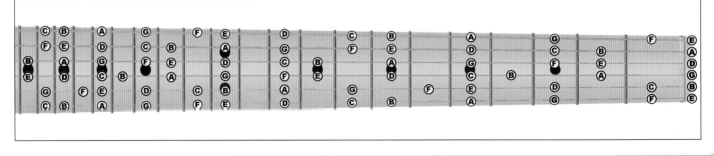

Continuing round the circle shows that each key has an incremental number of sharps to it. C has none, G has one, D has two, A has three, E has four, B has five, F# has six, and C# has seven.

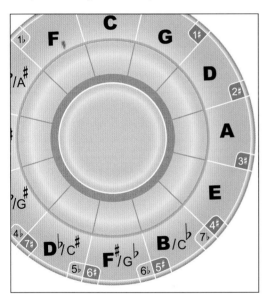

The circle can take us one step further by helping us to identify which notes are sharp in each key.

We know that in the G major key there is one sharp, the F#. If you check on the circle, this is the first sharp note clockwise from G. The D major scale has two sharp notes, F# and C#. As

you can see, the next sharp note clockwise on the circle from F# is C#. The pattern continues, using enharmonic equivalents where appropriate.

C has no sharps
G has 1 sharp: F#
D has 2 sharps: F# C#
A has 3 sharps: F# C# G#
E has 4 sharps: F# C# G# D#
B has 5 sharps: F# C# G# D# A#
F# has 6 sharps: F# C# G# D# A# E#
C# has 7 sharps: F# C# G# D# A# E# B#

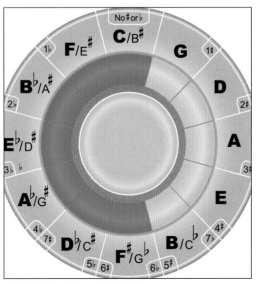

We can also use the circle to show us the scales with flat notes in them. If we move anti-clockwise from C we come to F. The scale of F has one flat note, Bb, which is the first flat note anti-clockwise from F.

C has no flats
F has 1 flat: Bb
Bb has 2 flats: Bb Eb
Eb has 3 flats: Bb Eb Ab
Ab has 4 flats: Bb Eb Ab Db
Db has 5 flats: Bb Eb Ab Db Gb
Gb has 6 flats: Bb Eb Ab Db Gb Cb
Cb has 7 flats: Bb Eb Ab Db Gb Cb Fb

In written music, unless otherwise indicated, the default key is C major, the only key without any sharp or flat notes. If music is written in any other key then the relevant number of sharps or flats is added to the beginning of the stave just after the clef, but before the time signature.

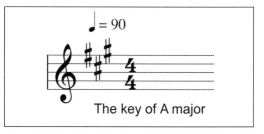

The key of A major

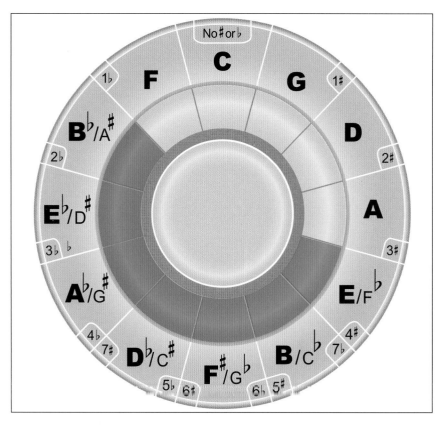

The sharps or flats are written on the stave in the order in which they appear in the key and on the correct line for the note. So, for example, if you see three sharp symbols at the beginning of a piece of music you know that it is in the key of A major. If you can't remember which notes are sharp in A major you can read them from their

Guitar tab

position on the stave and see that the F, C, and G are sharp. This means that all Fs, Cs, and Gs in the music should be treated as being sharps, regardless of the octave in which they appear.

Guitar tab, or tablature, is a relatively new way of writing guitar music that has its origins in medieval lute music and is a lot easier to learn than standard musical notation. It avoids the need for specialist music-creating software, as it allows music to be written using a basic text-editing or word-processing program, so it is often used to display music on the internet. However, because the music is specific to guitars, other musicians rarely understand it, and that can cause problems if you're playing in a band.

Tab doesn't indicate how long you should hold notes, so it is only useful for songs whose tune you are familiar with, and it also doesn't show which key the tune is in. As with standard musical notation, it doesn't show you which fingers to use to form the chords. Guitar tab, however, shows you what frets to play on each string, which makes it popular with beginners. Guitar tab is displayed as six parallel lines representing the six strings of the guitar. The top line is the top E string. The word TAB is often written vertically across the lines.

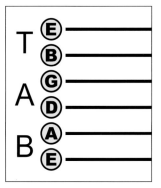

Numbers are written directly onto the lines to indicate which fret to hold down. A zero is used if a string is to be played open and a line is left blank if a string is to be ignored.

To play the scale of G major from the bottom E string, it would be shown as follows:

Sometimes the spacing of notes can give an indication of how long the notes are to be played for. Some versions of guitar tab include note symbols above the numbers to show note values.

Chords are displayed with the fret numbers written directly above one another.

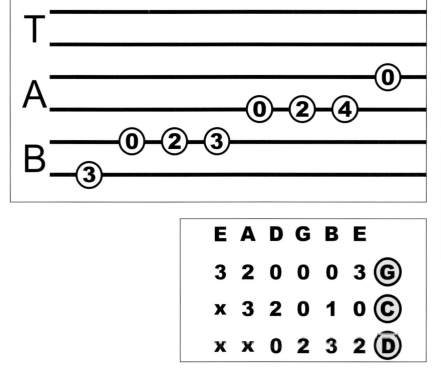

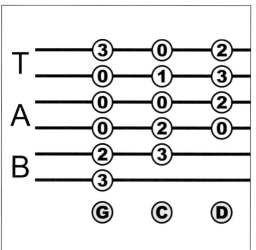

Sometimes chord sequences are simply written as lists of text ignoring the lines altogether. These lists are written horizontally with the strings written in the order of EADGBE. A zero still indicates an open string and an x is used to show a string is to be ignored.

When writing guitar tab using a computer, the lines for the strings are made up of hyphens. It is easiest to make a blank set of strings first using the hyphens, then copying and pasting them into another document. You shouldn't make the lines too long as they may wrap around the edge of the document onto the next line and ruin the layout. About 50 to 60 characters in length is about average. Also it is best to use a mono-space typeface such as Courier to type tab in, because most other typefaces give varied widths for different numbers and letters, which can also spoil the layout.

There are thousands of guitar tab tunes available for downloading from the Internet and you are likely to find some of your favorite tunes already written out in tab by someone else. However, you should bear in mind that many of these will be personal interpretations of the songs and may not be exact reproductions of the original music.

Tab works best when used alongside traditional notation and chord boxes, to give you as much information as possible.

Lead Guitar and Scales

Practicing scales is a good way to get to know the fretboard and should set you on the road to becoming a better player.

In this chapter we'll look at the most common scales in western music and get to understand how they are created.

Scales may sound rather boring but they are very useful and work particularly well on the guitar. You will soon learn which notes can be added to which chords to add color and texture to your playing.

Finding octaves

When tackling scales, it is essential to have a good knowledge of where the notes are on the guitar neck. This will enable you to move scale patterns around the neck to fit into different keys. Have another look at where the notes are to refresh your memory.

An important ability you need to have is to be able to find an octave of a particular note quickly. This is quite easy to do on the guitar as it follows simple patterns.

To find a note that is an octave higher than the original on the bottom E and A strings, you move up the guitar neck by two strings and two frets. This means that to find an octave of G on the 3rd fret of the bottom E string, you move up two strings to the D string and along the neck by two frets to the 5th fret.

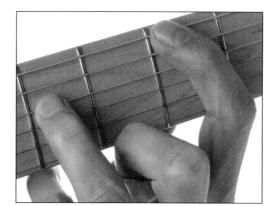

Right: Playing octaves from the bottom E string

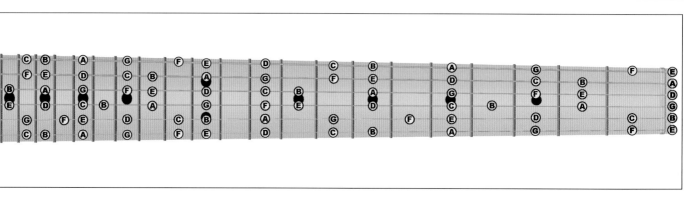

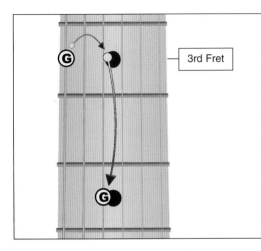

3rd Fret

This pattern works for any note on the two bottom strings.

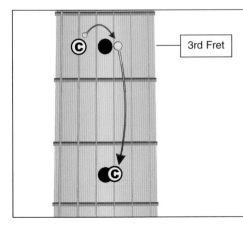

3rd Fret

To find the octave up from the D and G strings the pattern changes slightly. You move two strings up and three frets along. To find an octave from the E that lies on the 2nd fret of the D string you move up two strings to the B string and then along by three frets to the 5th fret.

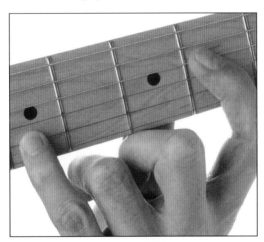

Again this pattern works for every note that lies along the D and G strings.

Left: Playing octaves from the D string

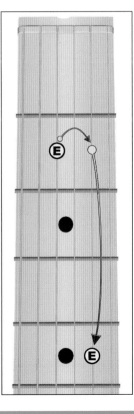

Right: Playing octaves from the top E string

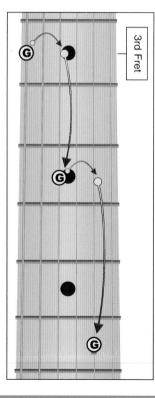

3rd Fret

Combining these two patterns will enable you to find two octaves' worth of notes quickly. If we look at the G again, the first G is on the 3rd fret of the bottom E string, the second G, one octave higher, is on the 5th fret of the D string and the third G, two octaves higher than the original, is on the 8th fret of the B string.

To work out the octaves going down from the high strings, there is a similar pattern. To find an octave down from the top E and B strings you move three strings down and two frets up.

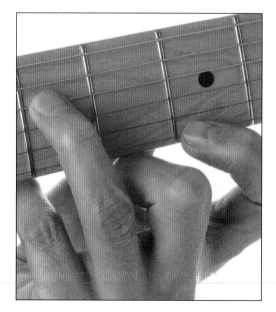

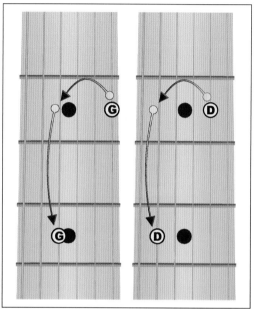

Being able to find the octaves of any note quickly will help you to learn where all the notes on the fretboard are. By learning all the notes of the bottom E and A strings, first you will soon be able to work out and recognize the location of notes on the other strings by using the patterns for octaves.

As an exercise, try to pick any note at random on the neck and see how long it takes you to work out what note it is.

Chromatic scale

All the scales we have looked at so far have been either major or minor ones that contain seven notes. Not all scales have seven notes to them, some have more and some have less.

The first scale we shall look at here has twelve notes and covers the entire range of possible notes. It is called the "chromatic scale" and it moves in semitones or single frets. Although this scale won't prove to be very useful when trying to devise solos, it is a useful exercise for your fingers and will show you how good finger placement will improve the fluidity of your playing.

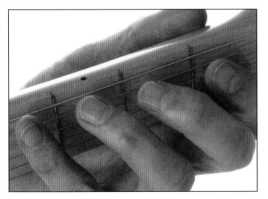

We will play the chromatic scale starting from the open E on the bottom E string and go through all the notes and frets until we reach the top E string and then go back again.

The most efficient way to play scales on the guitar is to try to use one finger for each fret covering a span of four frets. Try doing this on just the bottom E string first. Hold your left hand so that each of your fingers is just above a fret, the index finger over the 1st fret, and the second finger over the 2nd fret, the third finger over the 3rd fret, and the fourth over the 4th.

Strike the bottom E string five times, placing one finger after another on the frets so that you play through the notes E F F# G G#. Then try this in the reverse direction, lifting one finger at a time from the frets.

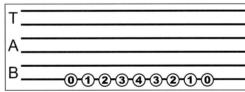

Play this forward and back a few times to get used to the feeling of placing and lifting the fingers sequentially. Try to keep the timing even and constant between the notes and try to strike the notes cleanly. You should hold your fingers only a short distance away when they are not pressing the strings, as this will enable you to perform this exercise much more quickly. Try to keep the fingers relaxed as your finger movement and reactions will be much faster.

Left: Placing the fingers over the first four frets

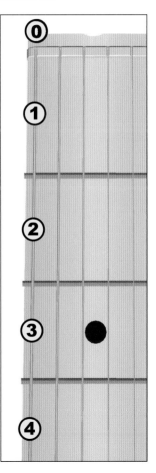

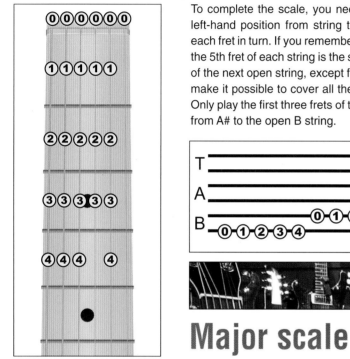

To complete the scale, you need to move your left-hand position from string to string, playing each fret in turn. If you remember that the note at the 5th fret of each string is the same as the note of the next open string, except for the G, this will make it possible to cover all the notes required. Only play the first three frets of the G string to go from A# to the open B string.

Once you get to the top, work your way back down again. Repeat this over and over, keeping the timing even but gradually try to increase the speed at which you work. After some practice, try to do it without watching your left hand.

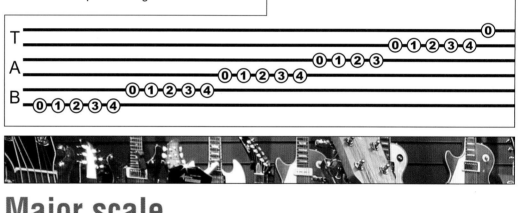

Major scale

The major scale is the most important scale to learn. Knowing this scale will make learning any other scale much easier, as you will be able to relate them in terms of changes made to the major scale. Also, knowing a major scale means that you will also know the scale of its relative minor, since they both use the same notes.

Before starting to play a major scale, let's look again at the relationships between notes, scales, and keys, to make sure we really understand what's going on in them. Let's look at the C major scale as it doesn't have any sharp or flat notes in it, although what follows applies to any scale.

C major scale

A major scale is defined by the pattern of intervals or spaces between the notes. This pattern is: Tone, Tone, Semitone, Tone, Tone, Tone, Semitone. A semitone is one fret space. In the case of C major this gives us the notes C D E F G A B C.

The chords that make up a major key also follow a pattern. This pattern is: Major, Minor, Minor, Major, Major, Minor, Diminished. In the case of C major it gives us the chords: C major, D minor, E minor, F major, G major, A minor, B diminished.

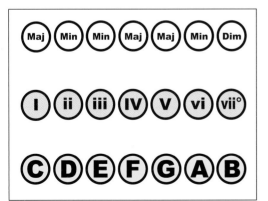

One important point to learn is that all of these chords are made up of notes from the C major scale. For instance, the D minor chord is made up of D, F and A, while B diminished is made up of B, D and F.

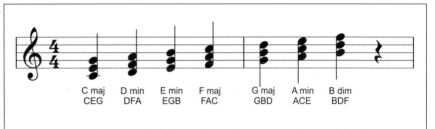

This becomes relevant when you want to play a solo. If you have a tune that uses any of these chords and you want to play a solo over it, you can use the notes of the C major scale and it will fit perfectly. Conversely, if you know the scale well enough, you will be able to pick out all the chords that lie within it.

Diatonic chords

Chords that use notes from another scale are said to be "diatonic" to the key. This means that all the chords in the C major key are diatonic apart from the C major chord itself, which is called a tonic chord.

G major scale

Let's have a look at another scale. This time we'll use the G major scale. This has the notes G (T), A (T), B (S), C (T), D (T), E (T), F# (S), G.

forward and backward a few times to get used to how it feels.

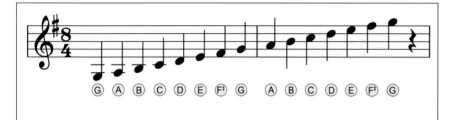

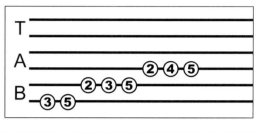

Therefore, the chords in the key of G major are: G major, A minor, B minor, C major, D major, E min, F# diminished. These chords are all made up from the notes of the G major scale.

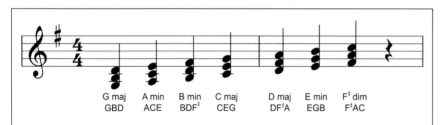

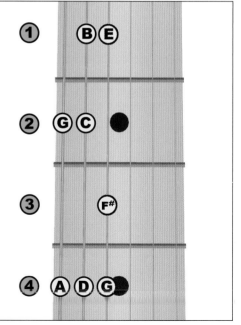

Let's now play the G major scale on the guitar to hear what it sounds like. Let's start playing from the G that is on the 3rd fret of the bottom E string. Use the one finger per fret rule that we used with the chromatic scale and start with the second finger on the G. Play this first octave

First scale pattern

Now we'll extend the scale by another octave and use all six strings. Still keep to the one finger per fret rule and play the scale back and forth until you feel comfortable with it.

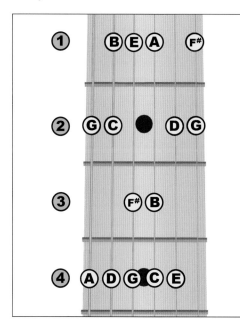

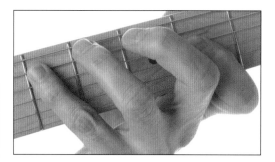

The pattern of notes that this makes across the fretboard is known as a scale pattern and is movable so that it forms a major scale from any note that lies along the bottom E string.

If you wanted to play the C major scale you would slide this pattern along to the 8th fret of the bottom E string.

Left: Playing the G major scale
Bottom Left: Playing the C major scale

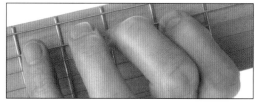

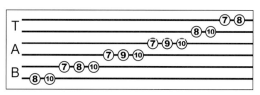

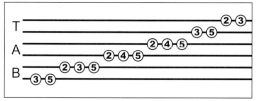

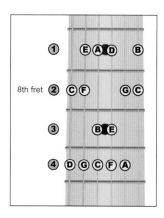

By moving this pattern around you can play every major scale on the guitar, even if you don't know all the notes. All you have to do is find the first/root note on the bottom E string.

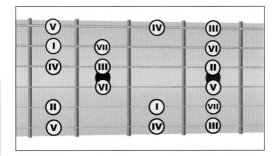

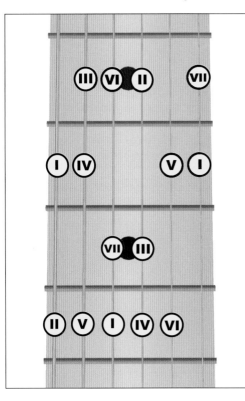

If we use this pattern to play the G major scale we would start at the 10th fret of the A string.

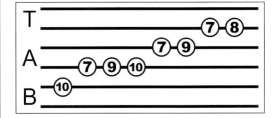

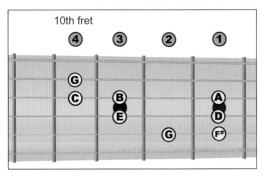

Let's look at another major scale pattern. This time, the root note is based along the A string.

Combining scale patterns

There may not seem to be much point in learning this new scale pattern when the one we have just learned works well, but have a look at what happens when we show both scale patterns at the same time.

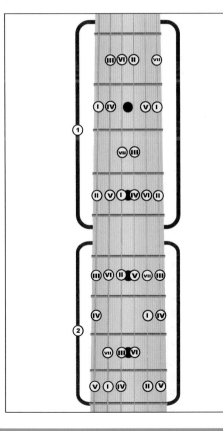

All the notes in the scale of G major appear on the neck. By combining these patterns, you can cover a longer range of the neck. You can also see alternative patterns that fall between the two that we have been practicing. You should begin to look for pathways that run across the two patterns. Try to keep to the "one finger per fret" rule as far as possible and occasionally slide the finger up the neck to reach other points.

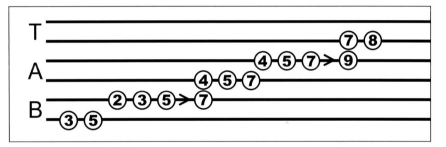

Try looking for alternative routes that go both up and down the neck. Also, try moving the patterns around the neck to practice different scales.

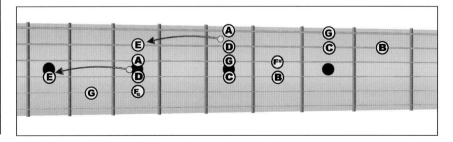

Third scale pattern

Right: Playing the third G major scale pattern

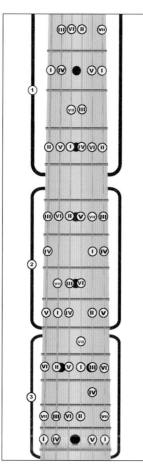

There is a third pattern that can be placed after the second one that will extend the range even higher up the neck. If you have difficulty reaching these notes on an acoustic guitar, you can drop the pattern back a couple of frets. If you are playing in G major, the pattern starts on the 15th fret of the bottom E string.

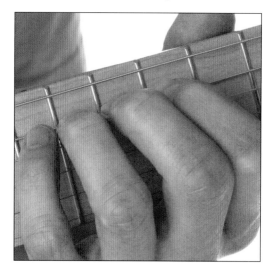

Combining all three scale patterns gives a map of almost the whole length of the neck. These three patterns work sequentially, so that if you have space on the neck you could place the first pattern after the third one, and so on. Or, if your root note starts higher up the neck, you could place the third pattern before the first.

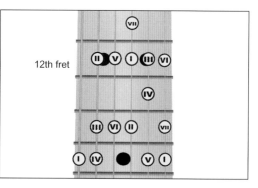

12th fret

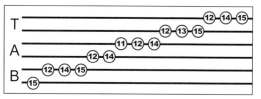

Spend some time practicing these scales and getting to know them. Move them around the neck so you are playing in different keys and pick paths through the map so that you can move up and down the neck.

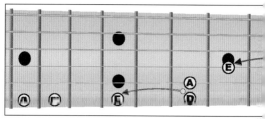

To create licks and runs, you have to start improvising around the scales, picking little patterns and runs that fit with whatever music you are playing along with. Generally, you should start and end your run with the same note, though not necessarily in the same octave. Try to start and end your run with the root note of whatever chord is playing at the time. So, for example, if you are playing a tune in the key of G major and you are using the I and IV chords which are G and D to make a riff, you can build a run that starts and ends with a G, the I or root note. Alternatively, you could build a run in D, starting and ending with the V note in the scale pattern, which may sound more interesting. If you know what chords are playing in the riff, it's easy to know where you can start your runs.

Using the scale patterns we created in G major, try the following exercise to hear how starting in different positions of the scale works with chords. We will use the I, IV, V, and vi chords from G major, the G, C, D and Em chords. Strum the chord, then play a run starting with the root note of the chord, but stick to the scale pattern of G major. Strum the chord again at the end of the run. Play the run in both directions.

Licks, runs, and riffs

A lick or run is a short lead solo used to punctuate or accent the music and can be used as a launch point for a full solo.

A riff is a short rhythm-based musical phrase that is repeated a number of times.

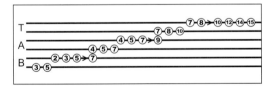

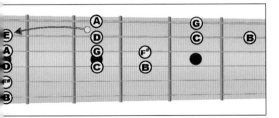

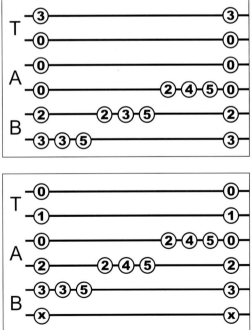

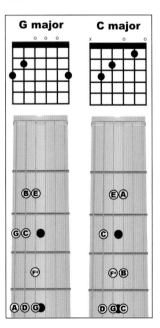

G major   C major

Modal scales

Moving the scales around so that they start with a different note is referred to as using "modal scales." Each starting point through the scale has a special name that comes from Ancient Greek.

I	T T S T T T S
	Ionian (major)
II	T S T T T S T
	Dorian
III	S T T T S T T
	Phrygian
IV	T T T S T T S
	Lydian
V	T T S T T S T
	Mixolydian
VI	T S T T S T T
	Aeolian (relative minor)
VII	S T T S T T T
	Locrian

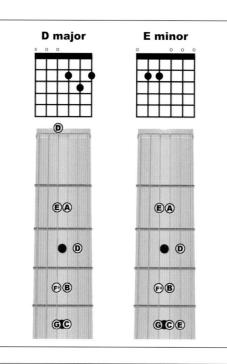

D major   E minor

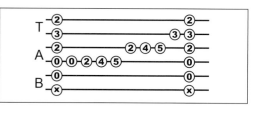

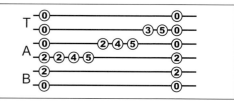

By learning the major scale patterns, you will know not only the scales of all the major keys, but also the patterns of all the relative minor keys as well, just by moving the starting point. When playing relative minor scales, it's best to try to imagine the VI position as being the root—keep the same pattern, just shift the numbering.

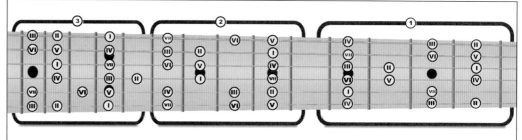

Facing Page: Playing the G major pentatonic scale

Pentatonic scales

If learning the major scale patterns seems too daunting a task, there is an alternative. You can use a stripped-down version of the major scale called the "pentatonic scale," which means a scale of five tones or notes. The major pentatonic scale leaves out the IV and VII notes from the normal major scale.

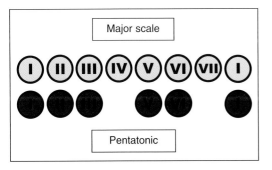

In the case of the G pentatonic scale, this leaves us with the notes G A B D E.

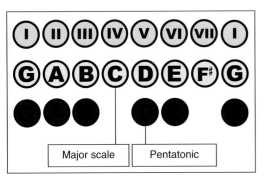

The reduced set of notes means that our scale patterns are less cluttered and simpler to remember. Ideally, you should remember the major scales and be able to leave out the IV and VII to play a pentatonic, rather than just learning a pentatonic scale.

Have a look at the reduced scale patterns for the pentatonic scale in G major.

You should practice playing through the scale and picking paths across the length of the neck. Try moving it to different positions so that you can play in other keys besides G major.

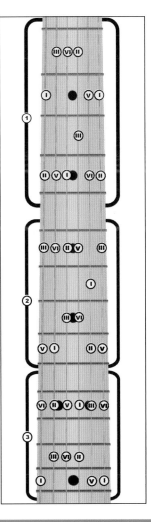

Blues scales

The blues scale is a variation on the pentatonic scale. It adds a flattened III note to the major scale or a flattened V if you are playing in a minor relative key. This flattened note is another so-called "blue note." This scale will give a blues feel to your solos.

The pentatonic scale doesn't work so well if you have included IV and vii° chords in your song, because it doesn't include the root notes in the scale.

You can still use modal scales to start the scale from a different note. So if you start from position VI you have the relative minor pentatonic scale.

You shouldn't get confused with the numbering, as we are still playing exactly the same notes, but just renumbering them from a new starting position, as though we were playing in E minor.

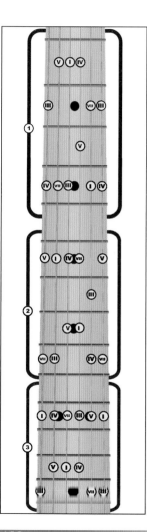

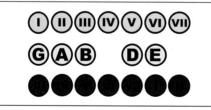

The third pentatonic scale pattern is perhaps the most useful as it is the easiest to play.

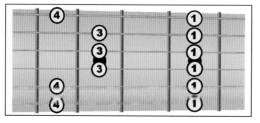

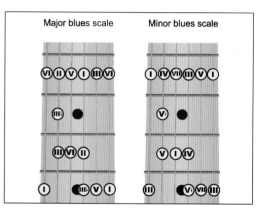

Major blues scale   Minor blues scale

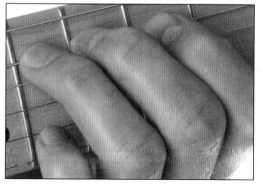

Minor scales

Melodic minor scales

The relative minor scales we have looked at so far are all called "natural minor scales" as they all use the same notes as their relative major scales. There are some other minor scales that have some variation to the notes in them.

The melodic minor scale has two parts to it. It is slightly different going up the scale from coming down it. The descending scale is the same as the natural minor scale that we have been using, but going up the scale the notes at position VI and VII are sharpened.

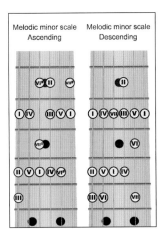

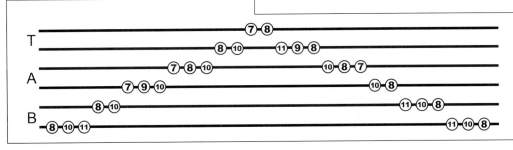

Facing Page: Playing the blues scale

Left: Playing the harmonic minor scale

Harmonic minor scale

The harmonic minor scale is the same both up and down. It is basically a natural minor scale with a sharpened VII note.

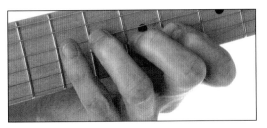

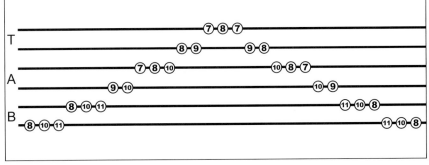

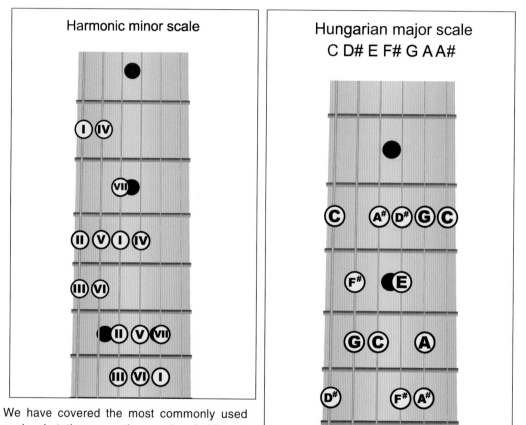

Harmonic minor scale

Hungarian major scale
C D# E F# G A A#

We have covered the most commonly used scales but there are thousands of different scales from all over the world, which you can find in books, if you are interested in scales. Here are a few unusual scales to give you a taster of some alternatives. They are all in the key of C.

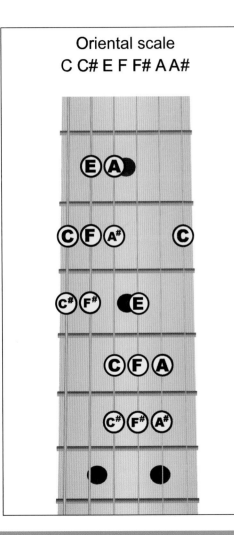

Oriental scale
C C# E F F# A A#

The way to achieve success in playing the guitar is to spend time practicing and learning the scales and keys. Then when jamming with a band or friends, you should let your instincts and reactions take over. You shouldn't be afraid to bend or break a few rules, as it will lead you to your own unique sound.

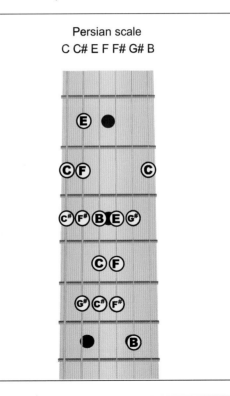

Persian scale
C C# E F F# G# B

Guitars, Amps, and Effects

If you become serious about playing the guitar, it's likely that you may want more than one. The different sounds produced by the different types of guitar may mean you want more than one so that you can experiment with a wider range of music. This chapter looks at what you should consider when buying a guitar.

We'll look at the main types of amps and speakers available for guitarists and help you to recognize which ones suit which purpose.

We'll also cover effects pedals and units, looking at classic effects as well as some of the newer multi-effect machines.

We'll finish off by looking at ways of recording your efforts and the options available for practicing alone.

Beginners' guitars

If you haven't already bought your first guitar to learn with, there are a few pieces of advice that you should take on-board. The most important, but simplest, advice is to buy the best guitar that you can afford.

When first starting to play, your fingers will be soft and not used to holding difficult chord positions. A cheap guitar may have a high action, where the strings are high above the fretboard, and poor sound, which is likely to impede your progress and make you work harder to achieve the desired results. This increases the likelihood of you giving up before you have made much progress.

The main objective for a beginner is to feel comfortable with the guitar. Balance and weight are easily checked but the action is also very important. If this is too high, then your fingers are going to have to press much harder on the strings than is normal and fatigue is likely to set in much quicker. If it is too low, then the strings and frets will buzz.

A good tone to the sound of the guitar really helps when starting out and will encourage you to progress. Cheap guitars usually sound cheap and can be frustrating for beginners, as it takes a skilled guitarist to make a cheap guitar sound good.

A guitar should be viewed as an investment, as good ones that are well looked after tend to hold their value and can even increase in value over long periods of time. Cheap guitars lose their value fairly quickly. There may not visually be much difference between a $200 guitar and a $2,000 one, but there will be a big difference in the quality of the materials used to make it. Good quality wood makes a big difference to the sound and feel of a guitar, while being hand-assembled rather than rolling off a factory production line will have a huge effect on the quality.

Right: Fender *Stratocasters*

Good quality guitars are made from expensive, and sometimes rare, woods, while cheaper guitars are made of plywood and have a thin veneer of more attractive or better quality wood on the surface. These cheaper guitars are unlikely to age very well.

When buying your first instrument, it is probably best to go for a steel-strung acoustic guitar so that you won't have to spend some of your budget on an amplifier as well. An acoustic guitar can be picked up and played immediately and the volume of your playing shouldn't disturb too many people while you're learning.

If you do decide to go for an electric guitar you may want to buy a small, headphone-based amplifier to use with it. However, you should be aware that extensive use of headphones might damage your hearing. As a musician, your hearing is of the utmost importance, so you should look after it. If you want to plug your electric guitar into your hi-fi system you will need a line-mixer to make them compatible.

Second-hand guitars are worth considering, as you are likely to get a much better deal for your money, than buying a new one for the same price and there are plenty of good deals and bargains around. Some of the best bargains are from people who have bought a guitar to learn with, but decide after a few months that they no longer want to play.

It is safer to buy a second-hand guitar from a guitar store rather than over the internet or from the classified advertisements in a newspaper, as the guitar store will have checked and serviced the instrument. You are also likely to be able to use the store for after-sales service if you need to. If you buy privately, try to get an experienced guitarist to look over the guitar for you. Look for an instrument that has been gently worn rather than been handled roughly. The tone on an aged guitar will have matured and the neck will have settled. A new guitar's tone will change as it adapts to its new environment.

Left: A Music Man Axis Super Sport

Extending your collection

Even if you have already bought a guitar, once you start making progress with your playing you may decide that you want to invest in another model.

You should think about what you want the new guitar for. Do you just want a better version of the one you already have or are you looking for some variety and to extend your guitar collection? It makes sense to buy an electric guitar for your second purchase if you already have an acoustic one and vice versa. An acoustic guitar is great to use at home, but if you want to play in a band or along with other musicians, you are probably going to need an electric guitar.

If you are looking to extend your collection of electric guitars, depending on what you already own, you may want one suited to playing lead guitar, such as a *Stratocaster* or a *Les Paul*, or one designed for playing rhythm such as a *Telecaster*. Alternatively, you may want to buy a semi-acoustic guitar instead.

Also, think carefully about where you will be using the guitar, at home, in a studio, or at gigs. Studio guitars will need quiet and clean sounding pickups and switches, while gig guitars will need to be able to stand up to some degree of rough treatment. Guitars bought for home use do not need to be so practical and can be collected for their own sake, so looks and history can be more of a consideration.

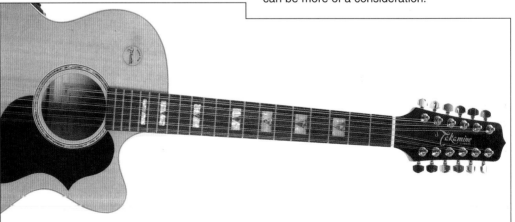

Right. A Takamine 12-string acoustic

Tips for buying guitars

Before you even begin to look for a guitar, it is best to decide on your budget and then stick to it. Otherwise it is easy to get swayed by the various, more expensive, models for sale. Visit a few guitar stores to get an idea of price ranges.

Take plenty of time when buying a guitar, as you may make the wrong decision if you buy on impulse. You are probably going to use your new acquisition for many years, so spending a few weeks making up your mind and trying alternatives will help confirm you have made the right choice. If you are worried that the guitar that you are interested in might be sold while you look around for others, you may be able to put down a deposit to show you are serious about buying it.

You should spend some time handling the guitar, as well as looking at it. Pick it up and hold it, trying it for weight, balance, and comfort. Ask to try it out and spend some time playing it or ask a guitarist to go with you to give you their opinion. When trying out the guitars, play through all the frets and strings to check for buzzing and ask about having adjustments made if you hear any. Try out all the knobs and switches to check they work well and don't produce any crackles.

If you are buying a second-hand model make sure that the strings aren't too old and dull when trying out the guitar. You may want to ask for new strings if you think it's necessary, as strings will affect the tone of the guitar. You should even consider paying to have a new set of strings put on if you think you might want to buy the guitar, as a few dollars spent before the purchase could save you from making a costly mistake.

When buying a guitar second-hand, you need to look for dents and scratches that may be signs of a poorly cared-for guitar. Dents along the neck or bent machine heads may be signs that the guitar has been dropped or knocked over and the neck will need careful checking. Look for chips and cracks in the varnish of the body if it is an acoustic guitar and watch out for loose struts inside the body, as these will affect the tone. If you can't see inside the body, tap lightly on it to listen for movement.

Right: Left-handed Gibson SGs

The neck is usually the main area of concern with second-hand guitars. Check all the frets to make sure they are not too worn or loose and in need of re-fretting.

Hold the guitar up and look straight down the length of the neck to see if there are any twists or bends in it. The neck should be straight. If the neck bends backward or forward, it will affect the action, but an engineer may be able to straighten it by adjusting the truss rod. If there is a double bend, or if the neck twists from side-to-side, you shouldn't buy the guitar.

Have a close look at where the neck joins the body, as this is where the most stress is placed. You should check for any bumps or humps in the body, which may indicate that the pressure on it is too great. Check that the machine heads turn smoothly and evenly and are not bent at all. Also, check that the bridge has room for adjustment, because although the action may be fine now, you may need to make adjustments in the future.

Most problems with guitars can be fixed, even cracked bodies and twisted necks, but you should factor in the cost of these repairs when negotiating a price and deciding whether the guitar is worth repairing.

It is advisable to avoid buying twelve-string guitars second-hand, because, due to the increased tension on their necks, their life span tends to be much shorter than that of six-string guitars.

It is worth finding a good, local guitar store if you can. If you are fortunate enough to have more than one, you should spend some time checking them out and asking questions to find out which store clerks give a good service and those you can trust for honest answers.

Right: Look down the neck for twists and bends

Amplifiers

It is best to buy from a dedicated guitar store, rather than a chain or department store. A small store tends not to be so concerned with making a quick sale, as the owners rely on the long-term benefits of having customers return to them, even if it is just for restringing.

Another advantage to buying from a dedicated guitar store is that guitars need to be set up and adjusted before they are displayed for sale and it is best to buy from somewhere with access to a workshop and an engineer who can make these adjustments. You should also take into account the after-sales options. Do you have a cooling-off period, during which you can return the guitar for a full refund if it turns out not to be the one for you? Also, consider whether the store offers setup and servicing, as you may well want to make small adjustments to fit in with your individual playing style.

If you have an electric guitar, you are going to need an amplifier to go with it. Not only is this an extra expense that you need to budget for, but it also means extra bulk. How much you can afford to spend on this piece of equipment may not be as important a consideration as how much space you have for storing it or how you are going to transport it.

Amps come in all sorts of sizes and power ratings, though they fall into two main categories: separates and combos.

Separates

When the amplifier is housed in one box and the speakers are in separate boxes, this is referred to as "separates." The amp allows you to connect to one or more speaker boxes via cables and usually allows you to connect to further amps so that you can connect to more speakers to create a louder sound. The power of sound that these stacks of speakers put out takes some time to get used to, as even a light touch of the guitar can be amplified to immense levels.

The problem of feedback, a howling scream-like noise from the speakers, occurs when the guitar

Left: A dedicated guitar store display
Above: An Orange stack

Combos

pickups start to pick up the sound coming from the speakers, then amplify it, and feed it back through the speakers ready to be picked up by the guitar pickups again.

The advantage of using separates is that they have a modular configuration, so you can add to them according to the size of the location where you will be playing. The problem is that they take up a lot of space and you may need to hire some roadies and a truck to transport them. A major consideration has to be whether you have the space to use them. The more speakers you use, the bigger the space needed to hear them properly.

Before deciding on a stack system, you should look at the size of the venues where you will be playing and rehearsing, to see if they will support such a big sound. Also, if you are playing in a band, you should take into account the equipment used by the other band members and whether they will be able to balance out the sound. If there are unlikely to be many occasions when you will need a very powerful sound you may want to hire the equipment instead.

Combos are combination amps, in which the amp and speakers are housed together in one box. This enables them to be stored and transported easily, making them very popular with guitarists.

Combos come in different sizes, from small amps used for practice to those used at gigs. The size of combo you choose will depend on what you are going to use it for. If it is just for practicing at home, then a small box will probably be sufficient. However, if you are going to be playing lots of gigs, then you will need something that can bring you up to the volume levels of the other instruments in the band. Many combo amps can take added speakers or another amp. Some combo amps have direct injection (DI) sockets, which allow sound engineers to take a direct signal from the amp to plug straight into a PA system. It is also possible to place a microphone in front of an amp's speakers to boost the volume through the PA system.

Right: Combo amps

Power

Amplifiers are rated by their power capacity, with bigger numbers meaning louder volumes. When checking the power rating of amps, you should look for the RMS (root means square) number to be able to compare one with another, as other measurements of power may be misleading. Power is measured in watts—the higher the wattage rating, the louder the sound the amp will produce. However, the wattage rating is only a rough indication of the power of the amp, as its design and construction and the type of speakers used will also affect the volume. The volume level of one 30-watt amp may be significantly different from another made by a different manufacturer. Generally speaking, a 15- to 30-watt amp will probably be sufficient for home use, whereas 60- to 100-watt amps will allow you to be heard at gigs, but are likely to make you unpopular if used at home.

Due to the way they are designed, amps work best when they are turned up above half way and you will often find the quality of sound will change significantly at different volume settings. So if you are playing a gig, it is important to practice at the volume level that you will be playing at. All amps come equipped with volume and tone controls. The tone control can range from basic bass and treble rotary knobs to sophisticated graphic equalizers that allow for more precise control over specific frequencies.

Some amps also have special effects built into them for more unusual sounds, but it may be better to spend more money on a better amp without these extra features and use an external effects box when you need one.

Tube amps

There are two main types of amplifier design: vacuum tube amps and solid-state amps. Originally, all amps were tube amps. Vacuum tubes are glass tubes containing filaments in a vacuum that glow when power flows through them, similar to light bulbs. Tubes have a tendency to distort and overdrive a signal as it passes through them, creating a rich, warm sound when used in a guitar amp. Tubes take time to warm up to reach optimum performance; they are also fragile and wear out with use.

Left: Vacuum tubes

Solid-state amps

In the Seventies, solid-state amps began to replace vacuum tube amps. The solid-state amps were much cheaper to produce, using printed circuit boards and transistors to power them. They produced a clean and reliable sound and allowed for more variety in sound settings. Gradually, though, many guitarists returned to tube amps, preferring the warm, overdriven sound characteristic of the valves.

Today, many amps are solid state with a vacuum tube output section, keeping the characteristic sound of the tube amps, but with the reliability and consistency of solid-state amps. Amps containing tubes tend to be more expensive than those without.

Speakers

Speakers come in many different sizes and, as with amps, their power rating is measured in watts. You need to match the power rating of your speakers to that of your amp. It's fine to have speakers with a higher power rating than the amp, but if it is less than that of the amp, you will damage the speakers when the amp is turned up fully.

The higher the power rating of a speaker, the more power it uses to convert into sound. Speakers do this by charging a magnet at the rear of the speaker and this pushes a coil in the cone of the speaker back and forth to move air and create sound. The size of the magnet and the quality of the cone has an effect on the sound. Bigger and heavier magnets usually mean better quality speakers.

Speakers are usually referred to by the size of the diameter of the speaker cone and are measured in inches. The size of the speaker cone does not affect the volume but it can affect the tone. Smaller speakers do not produce as many bass frequencies as larger ones, but the larger the speaker size, the further away from it you need to be before you can hear all the frequencies.

Common speaker sizes are 10", 12", 15", and 18", although the 18" are usually reserved for

bass amps. Speaker cabinets normally have groups of speakers wired together inside them. Combos tend to have pairs of speakers inside them such as two 10" speakers, while stack speaker cabinets tend to have groups of four such as four 12" speakers.

A good combination could consist of a combo with 10" speakers for rehearsals and monitoring your own stage sound and then an external box of 12" speakers to throw the sound out into a venue for live gigs.Speakers tend to wear out with age and use, so care must be taken to protect them from damage. It's best to touch the speaker cones as little as possible, because any damage such as holes or tears will affect the quality of sound.

Right: A speaker cone
Facing Page Right: A Boss multi-effects pedal
Facing Page Far Right: Various stomp boxes

Acoustic amps

These days, a wide selection of amps are designed specifically for acoustic guitars. These tend to include circuitry especially designed to boost the tonal qualities of an acoustic guitar rather than to overdrive and distort the sound as with those designed for electric guitars. Acoustic guitars are more prone to feedback, so amps designed for them usually have some form of feedback suppression built into them.

Amps are one area where you can save money by buying second-hand, as they tend to have long life spans and usually have little damage, due to spending time hidden at the back of the stage. When buying second-hand, look for tears and damage to the cones and listen out for crackles or popping sounds when turning the knobs and switches. Also listen out for any hum produced by the amp when no instrument is plugged into it. You should try to buy an amp

from a store or person who will allow you to return after purchase, as it is difficult to assess an amp's suitability without testing it in a live or band situation.

Effects

If you are an electric guitarist, it is worth trying out some different effects, which add substance to a tune—as well as hide the occasional mistake!

Effects units come in a bewildering range of styles and boxes. Generally they are either stand-alone units with a foot switch to turn them on and off—known as stomp boxes—or as multi-effects boxes that are either controlled with the foot or can be operated by hand. Some are small enough to be attached to a guitar strap, while some modern effects units are computer-based and more suited to a studio environment.

Distortion and overdrive

These pedals emulate the effect of having a large amp setup fully turned up. They will give you a heavy rock sound without the need to turn everything up to the maximum level. The effects can be used for either subtle changes, such as emulating a tube amp or creating a noise in which the original guitar sound is virtually non-existent.

Delay and echo

These units introduce a delay to the guitar signal and can then repeat the signal a number of times. The speed of the delay and the number of times the signal is repeated are variable. These effects are often used in dub reggae music.

Flanger and phaser

These pedals create a similar sound to a wah wah pedal, but the effect is more extreme. At their maximum setting, they can produce a noise more like a plane flying than a guitar playing. The phaser is the subtler of the two and works by sweeping a filter across the frequencies. The flanger produces a more noticeable effect, by feeding a slightly delayed version of the original sound back in on itself. Both are commonly used by funk guitarists.

Reverb

This is a much subtler kind of delay. Reverb emulates what happens as sound bounces off walls in a room. The settings allow you to recreate the sound that would be produced in different-sized rooms, from a tiny box-room to a cavernous hall.

Wah wah

A wah wah pedal produces a classic effect and is little more than a parametric equalizer controlled by a pivoting foot pedal. As the pedal is raised and lowered, it sweeps through the frequencies with extreme boost and cut, producing a crying "wah" sound to the guitar. The distinctive sound it produces can be heard on many funk and reggae tunes.

Chorus

A chorus is another kind of delay that adds pitch shift or tuning to the signal. It can be used to make a six-string guitar sound more like a twelve-string one or it can create the sound of a chorus of guitars.

Effects units are plugged in between the guitar and the amp, so if you use too many units you may get increased background noise going into the amp, which is where a multi-effects unit may help. You should also consider the large number of batteries or transformers required to power all these units.

Here is a list of some of the most common and popular effects available and a brief description of what they do. Bear in mind that there are many variations of these basic effects.

Equalizer

Equalizers or EQs are enhanced tone controls that allow you to target a particular frequency and either boost or reduce it. The frequencies can be selected using a twisting knob control that sweeps through them called a parametric EQ. Otherwise, frequencies are selected with a range of slide controls, each set up for selecting individual frequencies. This is called a graphic EQ.

Right: Native Instruments' Guitar Rig is a computer based amps and effects unit

Portastudios and sequencers

A wide range of portable recording machines are available, allowing you to record your playing and progress. Most enable multi-tracking, which means you can record one instrument at a time, or multiple times using the same instrument, allowing you to build songs in layers rather than having to record everything at once. Some machines have built-in rhythms and backing tracks that you can play along with.

Multi-track recording and sequencing software for the computer is another option for recording your tunes, as most computers are powerful enough to allow for real-time recording and playback, and are a good alternative to portastudios, if you can cope with the technical challenge.

Apple's Garageband software is a good starting place for building tracks to play along with. However, if you want to have a set-up similar to what you would get in a recording studio, you will need a top-of-the-range computer with lots of memory and disk space. Emagic's Logic Audio and MOTU's Digital Performer are often used in studios.

Cables

Although they are not an effect, cables will play a huge part in the quality of the sound your guitar produces. The signals that are sent from your guitar and through the various boxes carry very small currents and high-quality cables should be used so that no signal level is lost.

Try not to use cables that are too long, as this will reduce the signal level. Cables should have good shielding qualities or you may pick up radio signals while playing. Change your guitar leads at least once a year as the strands that make up the cable can weaken and break. The metal strands can also tarnish in damp conditions and this will reduce the signal that travels through them and affect your output levels.

Synth guitars

Synthesizers are no longer limited to keyboards and there are a few guitars that have built-in synths. More common are MIDI guitars that have a special pickup that sends note information rather than sounds through a special cable in general MIDI format to a digital computer. The signal enables the control of samplers, synthesizers, and drum machines. In fact, MIDI can control a whole range of equipment, even lighting rigs and mixers!

Compressor

A compressor evens out the levels of the low and high sounds of the guitar and compresses them to give a more punchy sound. This can help distinguish the guitar from other instruments that occupy a similar range of frequencies.

Top Left: MOTU's Digital Performer, multi-track recording studio for the Macintosh computer
Bottom Left: Replace cables regularly

Chord Bank

On the following pages you will find a handy reference section showing chords for all twelve notes. The chords are laid out in alphabetical order and feature both major and minor versions along with their 7ths; these are the most commonly used chords. Remember that some notes have enharmonic equivalents, so that the chords for A# are the same as those for B♭.

The chord bank is followed by charts to help you work out more complex chords more easily.

The major scale chart shows all the notes in each major scale based on the notes of the Circle of Fifths and the chord chart shows which notes within the major scale are used to create each chord. Between the two charts you should be able to work out more than two hundred chords.

A	A7	Am	Am7	A#	A#7	A#m	A#m7
B	B7	Bm	Bm7	C	C7	Cm	Cm7
C#	C#7	C#m	C#m7	D	D7	Dm	Dm7

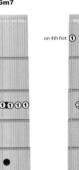
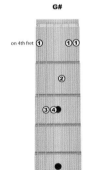

Chord	Major scale notes				
Major	1	3	5		
Minor	1	♭3	5		
Diminished	1	♭3	♭5		
Augmented	1	3	♯5		
Major 6th	1	3	5	6	
Minor 6th	1	♭3	5	6	
7th	1	3	5	♭7	
Major 7th	1	3	5	7	
Minor 7th	1	♭3	5	♭7	
Diminished 7th	1	♭3	♭5	♭♭7	
9th	1	3	5	♭7	9
7th + ♭9	1	3	5	♭7	♭9
7th + ♯9	1	3	5	♭7	♯9
11th	1	3	5	♭7	9	11
Augmented 11th	1	3	5	♭7	9	♯11
13th	1	3	5	♭7	9	13

The major scale chart lists all the scales based on the Circle of Fifths running down the left-hand side of the chart and shows the notes of each scale position along the top.

Remember that position eight is one octave higher than position one and that some of the notes have enharmonic equivalents.

The chord chart lists all the types of chords running down the left-hand side of the chart and shows which notes of the major scale are used to create them running along the side.

For example, if you want to create a F# major 6th chord, you look up the major 6th on the chord chart and see that it is made up of the 1st, 3rd, 5th, and 6th notes of the major scale. You then refer to the major scale chart and look up F#. Reading across the line you find that at these positions lie the notes F#, A#, C#, and D#. You then have to work out where these notes fall along the neck of the guitar to form the chord.

	1	2	3	4	5	6	7	8	9	10	11	12	13
A♭	A♭	B♭	C	D♭	E♭	F	G	A♭	B♭	C	D♭	E♭	F
A	A	B	C#	D	E	F#	G#	A	B	C#	D	E	F#
B♭	B♭	C	D	E♭	F	G	A	B♭	C	D	E♭	F	G
B	B	C#	D#	E	F#	G#	A#	B	C#	D#	E	F#	G#
C	C	D	E	F	G	A	B	C	D	E	F	G	A
D♭	D♭	E♭	F	G♭	A♭	B♭	C	D♭	E♭	F	G♭	A♭	B♭
D	D	E	F#	G	A	B	C#	D	E	F#	G	A	B
E♭	E♭	F	G	A♭	B♭	C	D	E♭	F	G	A♭	B♭	C
E	E	F#	G#	A	B	C#	D#	E	F#	G#	A	B	C#
F	F	G	A	B♭	C	D	E	F	G	A	B♭	C	D
F#	F#	G#	A#	B	C#	D#	E#	F#	G#	A#	B	C#	D#
G	G	A	B	C	D	E	F#	G	A	B	C	D	E

Glossary and Index